Series/Number 07-121

APPLIED CORRESPONDENCE ANALYSIS
An Introduction

STEN-ERIK CLAUSEN
Norwegian Institute for Urban and Regional Research

SAGE PUBLICATIONS
International Educational and Professional Publisher
Thousand Oaks   London   New Delhi

For information:

 SAGE Publications, Inc.
2455 Teller Road
Thousand Oaks, California 91320
E-mail: order@sagepub.com

SAGE Publications Ltd.
6 Bonhill Street
London EC2A 4PU
United Kingdom

SAGE Publications India Pvt. Ltd.
M-32 Market
Greater Kailash I
New Delhi 110 048 India

Printed in the United States of America

Library of Congress Cataloging-in-Publication Data

Clausen, Sten-Erik.
    Applied correspondence analysis: an introduction / Sten-Erik
Clausen.
        p. cm. — (Quantitative applications in the social sciences ; no. 121)
    Includes bibliographical references and index.
    ISBN 0-7619-1115-4 (pbk.: acid-free paper)
    1. Correspondence analysis. I. Title. II. Series: Sage university papers series.
Quantitative applications in the social sciences ; no. 07-121.
    QA278.5.C54   1998
    519.5′37—dc21   98-8883

                        04 10 9 8 7 6 5 4 3 2

Acquiring Editor:	C. Deborah Laughton
Editorial Assistant:	Eileen Carr
Production Editor:	Astrid Virding
Production Assistant:	Denise Santoyo
Typesetter:	Technical Typesetting Inc.

When citing a university paper, please use the proper form. Remember to cite the Sage University Paper series title and include the paper number. One of the following formats can be adapted (depending on the style manual used):

(1) CLAUSEN, S.-E. (1988) *Applied Correspondence Analysis: An Introduction*. Sage University Papers Series on Quantitative Applications in the Social Sciences, 07-121. Thousand Oaks, CA: Sage.

OR

(2) Clausen, S.-E. (1988). *Applied correspondence analysis: An introduction* (Sage University Papers Series on Quantitative Applications in the Social Sciences, series no. 07-121). Thousand Oaks, CA: Sage.

CONTENTS

SERIES EDITOR'S INTRODUCTION

Correspondence analysis, well-used by quantitative researchers in Europe, especially France, has not been much practiced in the United States. That is changing, partly due to the work of Greenacre and, earlier in this series, Weller and Romney (1990, *Metric Scaling: Correspondence Analysis*, No. 75). The monograph at hand, which emphasizes application and graphical interpretation, will further its spread. With the technique, the relationships among categorical variables in large tables can be summarily described. It maps the associations between rows and columns in a frequency table graphically, as points in a space of few dimensions. Conceptually, the analysis steps are simple. Category *profiles* (relative frequencies) and *masses* (marginal proportions) are computed, the distances between these points are calculated, and the best-fitting space of *n* dimensions are located. Rotation then occurs to maximize the *inertia* (variance) explained by each factor, as in principal components analysis. (On that technique, see Dunteman, *Principal Components Analysis*, No. 69 in this series).

The method is inductive, a search strategy for underlying structure within a data set. No distributional assumptions are necessary, unlike classical techniques involving inference to population parameters. Indeed, the only assumption required of the data is that the values not be negative. This exploratory procedure can be found in leading statistical packages, such as BMDP, SAS, or SPSS. Sten-Erik Clausen helpfully provides appendixes on appropriate programs from SAS and SPSS. Additionally, he includes a glossary of terms for the newcomer.

The explanations are lucid and economical. Further, they are sensitive to the treatment of particular difficulties, such as outliers, the number and meaning of dimensions. One concern he wrestles with is the tension between explaining much variance and achieving few dimensions. This and other dimensionality issues are similar to those faced in factor analysis and multidimensional scaling (see, respectively, Mueller and Kim, *Introduction to Factor Analysis*, No. 13; *Factor Analysis*, No. 14; and Kruskal and Wish, *Multidimensional Scaling*, No. 11).

Carefully chosen examples move students a long way down the road to understanding most research techniques. Here Clausen excels. The several illustrations are sequenced in order of difficulty and are based on various national surveys of obvious social policy relevance. The first relates leisure activities and occupation in two dimensions: one on arts and the other on age. In the space can be observed, among other things, manual workers close to disco dancers and professionals close to theater-goers. The second example looks at type of crime and place of residence. The third illustration examines the 1985 Health Survey of Norway, reducing a 12 × 6 × 2 matrix, or 144 cells, from three categorical variables on disease, age, and gender. The fourth scenario, inspired by the French sociologist Bourdieu, constructs the social space of welfare recipients using client type and demographic characteristics. It yields a two-dimensional map of relations among individuals where, for instance, one sees the "sick" grouping together at some distance from the "deviants." The fifth and final example comes from a Survey of the Level of Living in 1995. Focusing on gender, age, and alcohol consumption, Clausen demonstrates how correspondence analysis and loglinear models can be used jointly.

Analysts may have so many categorical variables that they are stymied by traditional tabular presentations. Especially if they want to simplify the variable complex and visually display an underlying data structure, they should turn to Clausen's cogent introduction to correspondence analysis applications.

—*Michael S. Lewis-Beck*
Series Editor

PREFACE

In 1987 I attended a conference on data analysis in Versailles, France. To my great surprise, the dominating theme at this conference was centered around a technique called correspondence analysis. I had never heard about it before, but soon realized that it was a very fascinating tool with which to describe the associations in large contigency tables. I immediately saw the need for an elementary introduction to this method for users outside France. This book is a contribution toward meeting that need.

First of all, I want to thank the Norwegian Institute for Urban and Regional Research, which has generously supported my work on this monograph. Since the topic was almost totally unknown in the Norwegian research milieus, work on this monograph has, in many ways, been a rather solitary process. However, I want to thank Trygve Kalve at Statistics Norway, who inspired me to translate and expand an earlier Norwegian version of this monograph. I also want to express my gratitude to Paul E. Spector and Herbert Weisberg for their fine comments and important suggestions for improvement on the first draft of this manuscript. I am grateful to the series editor, Michael Lewis-Beck, for his encouraging advice during my work on this monograph as well. Finally, I want to acknowledge Michael Greenacre, from whom I have learned correspondence analysis through his very readable writings on the subject.

Some of the data applied in this monograph are based on the *Health Survey 1985* and the *Survey of Level of Living 1995* conducted by Statistics Norway. Anonymized data sets have been made available by the Norwegian Social Science Data Services (NSD). Neither Statistics Norway nor NSD are responsible for the analyses/interpretations of data presented here.

To Stine, Janne and Liv

APPLIED CORRESPONDENCE ANALYSIS
An Introduction

STEN-ERIK CLAUSEN
Norwegian Institute for Urban and Regional Research

1. INTRODUCTION

The main purpose of this monograph is to provide a nontechnical introduction to simple correspondence analysis. It is intended for the general or applied social scientist, and does not presuppose any grounding in mathematics beyond elementary statistics. Correspondence analysis is a relatively unknown method of analysis within Anglo-American social sciences. The name is a translation of the French "analyse des correspondances," but the method is also referred to by other names such as "dual scaling," "additive scoring," "optimal scaling," "biplot," and "homogeneity analysis."

1.1. What Is Correspondence Analysis?

Correspondence analysis can be regarded as a special kind of canonical correlation analysis. This latter method analyzes the relations between two sets of continuous variables, whereas correspondence analysis analyzes the relations between the categories of two discrete variables. It is also possible, however, to analyze several variables simultaneously; for example, by transforming the matrix into a two-way table. This procedure is illustrated in Chapter 3.

The main purpose of correspondence analysis is to reveal the structure of a complex data matrix by replacing the raw data with a more simple data matrix without losing essential information. This implies removing "noise" or redundant information. Second, correspondence analysis makes it possible to present the result visually, that is, as points within a space, which facilitates interpretation.

Correspondence analysis is a method especially applicable for analyses of large contingency tables. The technique is a tool to analyze the *association* between two or more categorical variables by representing the categories of the variables as points in a low-dimensional space. Categories with similar distributions will be represented as points that are close in space, and categories that have very dissimilar distributions will be positioned far apart. An example will help clarify how this works. Table 1.1 shows a cross-classification of leisure activities (performed during the year up to the interview) with the respondents' occupational status.

By applying correspondence analysis to this table we get the geometrical display shown in Figure 1.1. The figure shows a two-dimensional joint space where the points represent the categories of the two variables. Such displays are often called maps. The result is interpreted on the basis of the relative positions of these points, for example, as spatial dimensions and/or clusterings. The number of dimensions is, at most, one less than the number of categories in the variable with fewest categories. As a rule, however, only a few of these dimensions will be interpretable or of substantial interest.

The two-dimensional display in Figure 1.1 may be interpreted as representing the association of the occupational categories with the different leisure activities. Details about how correspondence analysis functions will be presented in Chapter 2, but for the moment we may give the following interpretation of the results: The horizontal dimension separates the young (students) from the old (retired), and

TABLE 1.1

A Cross-Classification of Leisure Activities with Occupation
(*Survey of Level of Living 1995*, Statistics Norway)

Leisure Activities	Manual	Low N.M.[a]	High N.M.[a]	Farmer	Student	Retired
Sport events	301	497	208	50	254	187
Cinema	261	550	250	27	339	157
Dance/disco	361	534	204	59	324	216
Cafe/restaurant	463	766	334	72	350	601
Theater	89	350	195	12	143	167
Classical concert	23	182	124	10	60	110
Pop concert	117	298	145	11	184	56
Art exhibition	104	379	219	21	152	213
Library	130	352	153	17	272	264
Church service	168	370	187	51	162	424

[a]N.M., nonmanual.

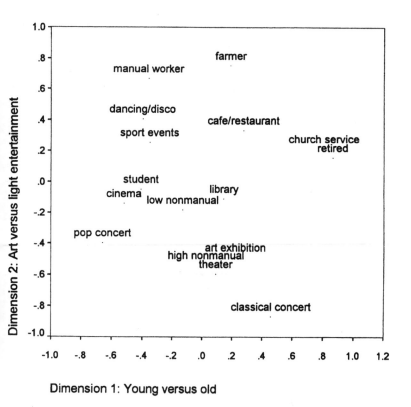

Figure 1.1. The Result of Correspondence Analysis Applied to Table 1.1. The Occupations and the Activities Are Represented as Points in a Two-Dimensional Space

the vertical dimension separates cultural activities from light entertainment. The positions of the points indicate that retired people are associated with church services and high status nonmanual occupations are associated with art exhibitions, theater-going, and classical concerts. Further, the display shows that students and low status nonmanual occupations are associated with the cinema and pop concerts, whereas manual workers and farmers are situated closer to light entertainment like dancing, sport events, and cafes/restaurants. This example should provide an intuitive understanding of the unique

4

property of correspondence analysis in visualizing the associations between categories in contingency tables.

The analytical process, which is explained in detail in the next chapter, is performed in two stages: first for the set of categories for one variable, and then for the set of categories for the other variable. Each stage can be divided into three steps, and the process is illustrated in Figure 1.2. The first step is to calculate the categorical profiles (i.e., the relative frequencies or conditional proportions) and masses (marginal proportions). The next step is to compute the distances between the points. The problem is then to find the n-dimensional space that best fits the points. The configuration is

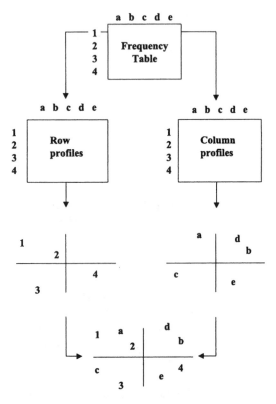

Figure 1.2. Illustration of the Three Stages in the Analytical Process of Correspondence Analysis (adapted from Greenacre, 1981)

rotated so that the variance explained by each factor is maximized in turn. This means that factor 1 explains most variance, then factor 2, and so on. This part of the analysis corresponds to principal component analysis.

1.2. The History of Correspondence Analysis

The development of correspondence analysis over time is somewhat confused since it has been developed and redeveloped by several scientists independently. This course of events is described in detail in Nishisato (1980). Only a few of the most important contributions to the development of the method are referred to in the following text.

Correspondence analysis fits into a tradition based on the works of Karl Pearson and, later, Hotelling's (1933) further development of principal component analysis. Today, Hirschfeld (1935) (also known as H. O. Hartley) is usually regarded as the founder of the method, but important pioneer works were also published by, for example, Fisher (1940) and Guttman (1941). Hirschfeld's and Fisher's works belong to what is often classified as the bivariate tradition, whereas Guttman worked within the multivariate tradition. Guttman (1941, 1950, 1959) presented a solution to the problems associated with the method, and it is interesting to note that his results were reproduced by others later on. This is partly because the work was going on simultaneously in several countries, for example, France, Japan, the Netherlands, and English-speaking countries (United States, England, Canada), and communication was hampered by language problems. This parallel development led to the establishment of a number of different schools or directions of correspondence analysis. However, in recent years, several works have been published with the objective of uniting the different variants of this method, for example, Gifi (1981) [a pseudonym for de Leeuw et al. (Young, 1984)] and Tenenhaus and Young (1985).

Correspondence analysis has been very popular in France, mainly owing to the efforts of Jean-Paul Benzécri and colleagues, which resulted in the publication of a large work on data analysis (Benzécri et al., 1973). The main reason why the work of this group is not better known among the more American-dominated research milieus is probably owing to a lack of knowledge of French. Correspondence analysis came to occupy such a strong position in the analysis methodology applied in France that it almost became synonymous with data analysis. The French tradition has placed special emphasis on the geometrical aspect, which has contributed to an affinity with multidimensional scaling and cluster analysis.

The work carried out by Benzécri and his colleagues can be said to represent a methodological philosophy based on inductive reasoning. By contrast to the traditional systems of analysis used to interpret categorical data, the method does not assume any underlying theoretical distribution. The main objective is to discover the structure inherent in the data. In other words, correspondence analysis is a model-free method where the data are not subject to any restrictions. This may not be quite correct, however, because certain choices have been made in choosing correspondence analysis, as in the kind of metric and weights used (van der Heijden, Mooijaart, and Takane, 1994).

The method has been used mainly as a technique for *exploratory data analysis*, like factor analysis and multidimensional scaling. It must be pointed out, however, that all these methods of analysis have developed techniques for hypothesis testing or confirmatory analyses (see, e.g., Fornell, 1982; Greenacre, 1984).

Very little has been published in English on correspondence analysis, and before 1970 there was only one such publication by Benzécri (1969). A breakthrough came with an article by Hill (1974). Since then, the method has been described in several books, for example, Nishisato (1980), de Leeuw (1984), Greenacre (1984), Lebart, Morineau, and Warwick (1984), and Benzécri (1992), but all of these books presented the method rather technically. More recent and less technical introductions are now available (Weller and Romney, 1990; Greenacre, 1993). Also some journal articles and chapters in edited books have presented the method in relatively elementary forms, including Greenacre (1981, 1994) and Hoffman and Franke (1986). For persons familiar with the French language, however, quite a large number of books are available describing the method in elementary terms, including Cibois (1983) and Legarde (1983). Figure 1.3 schematically presents important writings in English on correspondence analysis published since 1970. The figure shows the authors and the years of publication by country of origin. The shaded boxes refer to the least technical texts.

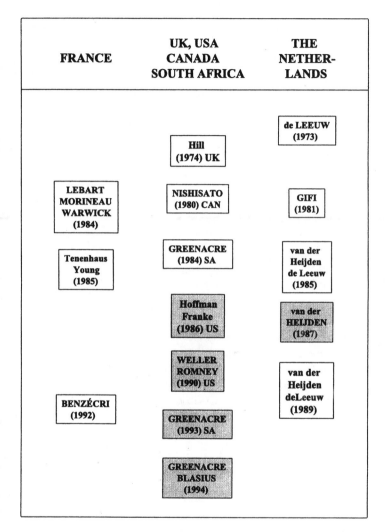

Figure 1.3. Schematic Presentation of Some Important Recent Writings in English on Correspondence Analysis. Small Letters Refer to Articles; Capital Letters Refer to Books; Shaded Boxes Represent the Least Technical Texts

There are signs that correspondence analysis is becoming more prevalent among American social scientists and students. Young (1984) included a special section on correspondence analysis in his general article on scaling. Moreover, Goodman (1987) showed how loglinear models, latent class analysis, and correspondence analysis are all related, and developed new methods based on these three methods in order to discover the metric information contained in qualitative variables. However, one of the major reasons for the increasing attention to correspondence analysis is the growing interest in the work of the French sociologist Pierre Bourdieu (see, e.g., Calhoun, LiPuma, and Postone, 1992), who has applied correspondence analysis in several works (e.g., Bourdieu, 1984, 1988).

Correspondence analysis is likely to receive more use since it is now included in several American statistical packages, such as BMDP (Moran and Gornbein, 1988), SPSS (SPSS Inc., 1990), and SAS (SAS Institute, 1989). The correspondence analyses presented in this monograph were originally performed with a program called CORAN (Lebart, Morineau, and Warwick, 1984), but have been reanalyzed with SAS and SPSS for this monograph (see Appendixes B and C).

Terminology

When reading about correspondence analysis, a problem often arises because different authors apply different terms to equivalent phenomena. In this text a vocabulary has been chosen to match the output of SAS and SPSS. The different terms will be defined in Chapter 2, and readers interested in equivalent terms are referred to the glossary in Appendix A.

2. THE ESSENTIALS OF CORRESPONDENCE ANALYSIS: A SIMPLE EXAMPLE

Let us now analyze the data in Table 2.1 step by step. The data have been taken from *Criminal Statistics 1984* (Statistics Norway, 1986) and show a cross-classification of crimes investigated by the police and different areas in Norway. Data were available for the entire country, but for illustrative purposes only three areas are shown. Likewise, only three types of all crimes investigated are shown: burglary, fraud, and vandalism. The advantages of the method are greatest, however, when it is used to analyze large tables.

The analysis is first carried out separately for rows and columns. Since the process is the same for both, we shall concentrate on rows only in this example. For the time being, we shall ignore the last two columns in the table, as well as the bottom row. We will make use of these data in Section 2.7.

2.1. Geometric Representation: Profiles, Masses, and Chi-Square Distances

The concepts to be discussed in this section are essential for understanding how correspondence analysis functions and how it is possible to transform a contingency table to a graphic or geometric representation. While reading, it might be helpful to refer back to Figure 1.2, which illustrates the whole analytical process in a single picture.

TABLE 2.1

Investigated Crimes by Type and Site of Crime, and Inhabitants (in Thousands) by Type of Residential Area

| | | | | | Residential Area | |
| | | | | | Dense | Sparse |
Part of Country	Burglary	Fraud	Vandalism	Total		
Oslo area	395	2,456	1,758	4,609	749	66
Mid Norway	147	153	916	1,216	235	135
North Norway	694	327	1,347	2,368	283	185
Total	1,236	2,936	4,021	8,193	1,131	297
Norway	4,558	5,129	10,842	20,529		

Profiles and Masses

The analysis starts by transforming the frequencies in a cross-classification into proportions, which, as far as the rows are concerned, gives a set of so-called *row profiles*. Both the row and column profiles are shown in Table 2.2, and the row profiles correspond to the relative frequency distributions of the different crimes for each part of the country. To illustrate, the row profile for Oslo is calculated in the following way: $395/4609 = 0.086$, $2456/4609 = 0.533$, and $1758/4609 = 0.381$. Multiplying these ratios by 100 gives the row percentages for Oslo. The table also shows the *average row profile*, which, in a similar way, is the profile of the *marginal* distribution of the column variable (type of crime). The last column in Table 2.2 shows the *row masses* or the marginal profile. These are composed of the relative frequency distributions of the sums of the rows (marginal distribution). Since each row profile is independent of the total number in the category concerned, the masses are used to provide information on this number. They can be said to be a measure of the importance of a particular profile in the analysis. Note that the row masses equal the average column profile and, correspondingly, the column masses equal the average row profile.

Each row profile may be regarded as a mathematical vector, and a vector may be represented as a point in space where each profile

TABLE 2.2
Profiles and Masses for the Data in Table 2.1

Part of Country	Row Profiles			Total	Row Masses
	Burglary	Fraud	Vandalism		
Oslo area	0.086	0.533	0.381	1.00	0.563
Mid Norway	0.121	0.126	0.753	1.00	0.148
North Norway	0.293	0.138	0.569	1.00	0.289
Average row profile	0.151	0.358	0.491	1.00	

	Column Profiles			Average Column Profile
Oslo area	0.320	0.837	0.437	0.563
Mid Norway	0.119	0.052	0.228	0.148
North Norway	0.561	0.111	0.335	0.289
Total	1.000	1.000	1.000	
Column masses	0.151	0.358	0.491	

element constitutes a coordinate in space. In this way, every row (and column) profile may be represented as points in a three-dimensional space. The more similar the profiles of two rows are, then the closer to each other will the points be placed in space. Correspondingly, two very different profiles will produce points lying far away from each other.

The average row profile is the total of numbers in the different columns divided by the total sum, and is the *weighted* average of the row profiles. This point is often called the *centroid* and it is placed at the origin of the principal axes. If a profile is very different from the average profile, then the point will lie far from the origin, whereas profiles that are close to the average will be represented by points close to the centroid. If all the categories have equal profiles, all the points will fall in the centroid.

Chi-Square Distances

The distance that we are familiar with and that corresponds to our everyday experiences is called *Euclidean distance*. These distances between points in space can be calculated by using the Pythagorean formula

$$s(i, i') = \sqrt{\sum_j (a_{ij} - a_{i'j})^2} \qquad (2.1)$$

By applying the row and column profiles in Table 2.2 we can calculate the Euclidean interpoint distances between the different areas and between the different crimes. To illustrate, the distance between Oslo area and mid Norway is calculated in the following way:

$$s = \sqrt{(0.086 - 0.121)^2 + (0.533 - 0.126)^2 + (0.381 - 0.753)^2}$$

$$= 0.553$$

The chi-square distance, however, is a *weighted* Euclidean distance, where the weight is the inverse of the respective average profile element. This implies that the categories with few observations contribute relatively more to the interpoint distances than categories with more observations (Greenacre, 1994). To calculate the distances between the different points we may apply the formula

$$d(i, i') = \sqrt{\sum_j \frac{(a_{ij} - a_{i'j})^2}{a_{\cdot j}}} \qquad (2.2)$$

where $d(i, i')$ is the chi-square distance between the points i and i', a_{ij} are elements in the row profile, and $a_{\cdot j}$ are elements in the average row profile.

By using Equation 2.2 we can calculate the chi-square distance between Oslo and mid-Norway:

$$d(1,2) = \sqrt{\frac{(0.086 - 0.121)^2}{0.151} + \frac{(0.533 - 0.126)^2}{0.358} + \frac{(0.381 - 0.753)^2}{0.491}}$$

$$d(1,2) = \sqrt{0.7526} \qquad d(1,2) = 0.868$$

The numerators contain, for each crime, the squared differences between the profile elements for Oslo and mid Norway, divided by the average profile element of the respective crime category (or multiplied by the inverse of the average profile element). Note that these distances can only be calculated between categories of the same variable, not between categories of different variables. This means that the distances between areas and between crimes are defined, but the distances between areas and crimes are not. Correspondence analysis is based on this chi-square metric and may be described as a technique for decomposing the chi-square statistic.

Geometric Representation

Table 2.3 shows the distances between the area points and the distances of the different points to the centroid or the origin of the axes. When similar calculations have been carried out for the columns, the remaining problem is to find the axes in the p-dimensional space that lie closest to all the points.

Using the figures in Table 2.3 it is now possible to plot the points in a two-dimensional space. Since there are three points, these can be described perfectly in two dimensions. This configuration of the points is illustrated in Figure 2.1. The next problem to be solved is to rotate the axis so that it lies as close as possible to the points. As a

TABLE 2.3

Interpoint Distances (d) and the Distances of the Points from
the Centroid (Shown by the Table's Diagonal)

Category	1	2	3
1. Oslo area	0.372		
2. Mid Norway	0.868	0.544	
3. North Norway	0.890	0.515	0.530

measure of closeness we use the weighted sum of the squared
distances (z^2) from the points to the axis, where the weights are the
row masses (r) given in Table 2.2. Thus the intention is to minimize
Σrz^2. This problem is the same as maximizing the weighted sum of
the squared coordinates (Σrf^2).

The problem is solved by means of principal component analysis,
and the result of this analysis provides a number of useful descriptive
statistics in addition to the graphical display. The results of this
analysis will now be presented. Figure 2.2 shows the two-dimensional
solution to the analysis of Table 2.1. The interpretation of such

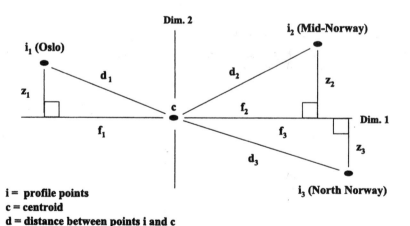

i = **profile points**
c = **centroid**
d = **distance between points i and c**
z = **distance between points i and the axis**
f = **coordinates**

Figure 2.1. Illustration of the Problem of Finding a Space That Lies Closest
to the Points

14

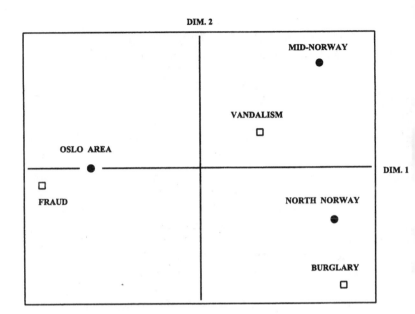

Figure 2.2. Graphical Display of the Results of the Analysis of Table 2.1, Without Supplementary Points

configurations will be discussed in more detail later. It is immediately obvious that the result, or display, shows three distinct clusterings, where each part of the country is grouped together with a particular type of crime. Relatively more fraud is investigated in the Oslo area, with relatively more vandalism and burglary in mid and north Norway, respectively.

2.2. Decomposition of Inertia

In correspondence analysis the *variance* concept is connected to the chi-square distances. Within this tradition the term *inertia* is often used, and hereafter the terms inertia and variance will be used as synonymous terms. *Total inertia* is a measure of the extent to which the profile points are spread around the centroid, and it is calculated by means of the formula

$$\Lambda^2 = \sum_i r_i d_i^2 \qquad (2.3)$$

where d_i is the point i's chi-square distance from the centroid and r_i is the point i's mass (weight). Using the values in Tables 2.2 and 2.3, we get

$$\Lambda^2 = 0.563(0.372^2) + 0.148(0.544^2) + 0.289(0.530^2) = 0.2029$$

Total inertia is directly related to Pearson's chi-square statistics as follows:

$$\chi^2 = \Lambda^2 N \qquad (2.4)$$

where N is the total number of observations in the table. In our example this gives

$$\chi^2 = 0.2029(8193) = 1662.6 \qquad \text{df} = 4$$

It can be seen from Equation 2.4 that also the total inertia (Λ^2) is like Pearson's contingency coefficient or phi-square ("coefficient of mean square contingency"):

$$\varphi^2 = \frac{\chi^2}{N} = \Lambda^2 \qquad (2.5)$$

Correspondence analysis can also be described as a technique for decomposing the phi-square (i.e., the deviation from independence) for a frequency table. First of all, the total inertia is decomposed into a set of eigenvalues.

Eigenvalues

The number of eigenvalues that are decomposed is equal to the total number of dimensions, which in turn is equal to the minimum of $(I - 1, J - 1)$, where I and J are the number of categories in the variables in the table. These eigenvalues express the relative importance of the dimensions or how large a share of the total inertia each

TABLE 2.4

Eigenvalues, Percent Inertia, and the Coordinates of the Points

	Dim. 1	Dim. 2	Sum
Eigenvalue (λ^2)	0.1774	0.0255	0.2029
Percent variance	87.4	12.6	100.0
		Coordinates	
Oslo area	-0.37	-0.01	
Mid Norway	0.42	0.35	
North Norway	0.51	-0.16	
Burglary	0.51	-0.33	
Fraud	-0.55	-0.05	
Vandalism	0.24	0.13	

of them explains. The shares are calculated so that the first dimension explains most, then the second, and so on.

Table 2.4 shows the eigenvalues for our data matrix. It is seen that the first dimension explains 87.4% of the inertia ($\lambda_1^2 = 0.1774$), whereas the second dimension explains the remaining share of 12.6% ($\lambda_2^2 = 0.0255$). In our example two dimensions are sufficient to explain the total inertia.

In the literature today we often find the term *singular values* used instead of eigenvalues. The singular value is the square root of the eigenvalue and is connected with one of the most useful tools used in matrix algebra ("singular value decomposition" or "basic structure"). This technique is described in Green and Carroll (1976) and Greenacre (1984).

2.3. Coordinates

The coordinates or scores provide information on the position of the points in relation to the dimensions, and are shown in Table 2.4. These are the values that provide the basis for the graphical display in Figure 2.2. The results are interpreted on the basis of the relative positions of the points and their distribution along the dimensions. In this solution the distances between the points within each set are the same as the chi-square distances, since the solution explains 100% of the total inertia. When analyzing large tables, often only a minor part of the inertia will be explained, and in such cases, the distances in the solution will only be approximations to the chi-square distances. *It is important to realize that it is only the distances within each set of points that are defined, not the distances between points from different sets or variables.*

The coordinates represent a decomposition of d^2 (the squared chi-square distance to the origin). We used d^2 before to calculate total inertia, and we can similarly use the coordinates of the points to find the eigenvalues of each dimension. We then use the formula

$$\lambda_k^2 = \sum_i r_i f_{ik}^2 \tag{2.6}$$

where f_{ik}^2 is the square of point i's coordinate on dimension k and r_i is point i's mass. For the first dimension this gives

$$\lambda^2 = 0.563(-0.37^2) + 0.148(0.42^2) + 0.289(0.51^2) = 0.1774$$

In order to obtain a more complete and correct interpretation of the results of the correspondence analysis, another two sets of descriptive statistics are used as well: *contribution of points to the inertia of dimensions* and *contribution of dimensions to the inertia of points*. These are often called absolute contributions and squared correlations, respectively.

2.4. Contribution of Points to Dimensions or Absolute Contributions

The contribution of points to dimensions is interpreted as the proportion inertia of a particular dimension explained by the point and it expresses the extent to which the point has contributed to determine the direction of the dimension concerned. These contributions are an aid in interpreting the dimensions, and points with relatively large contributions are most important to the dimension concerned. Within each set of points, the sum of these contributions for each dimension equals 1.00.

The contribution of points to dimensions are defined by the formula

$$ca_{ik} = \frac{r_i f_{ik}^2}{\lambda_k^2} \tag{2.7}$$

TABLE 2.5

The Contribution of Points to the Inertia of Each Dimension
(CONTR) and the Squared Correlations (CORR2)

Category Points	CONTR		CORR2		Quality Sum
	Dim. 1	Dim. 2	Dim. 1	Dim. 2	
Oslo area	0.436	0.002	0.999	0.001	1.00
Mid Norway	0.147	0.704	0.593	0.407	1.00
North Norway	0.417	0.294	0.908	0.092	1.00
Sum	1.000	1.000			
Norway			0.902	0.098	1.00
Burglary	0.223	0.627	0.712	0.288	1.00
Fraud	0.612	0.030	0.993	0.007	1.00
Vandalism	0.166	0.344	0.770	0.230	1.00
Sum	1.000	1.000			
Sparsely populated			0.973	0.027	1.00
Densely populated			0.176	0.824	1.00

where r_i is the mass of profile point i, f_{ik} is the coordinate of point i on dimension k, and λ_k^2 is the eigenvalue of dimension k. Since ca is a function of the mass and the coordinate of the point, this implies that the one can, to a certain extent, compensate the other.

The contributions of points are shown in Table 2.5 and it is seen, for example, that within the first set of points, the Oslo area and north Norway contribute about the same to the first dimension (43.6 and 41.7%, respectively), whereas mid Norway contributes most to the second dimension (70.4%).

If we take a look at the other set of points, type of crime, we see that dimension 1 is defined primarily by the category fraud and dimension 2 is defined by burglary. The category vandalism makes a smaller contribution to the dimensions, and Figure 2.2 shows that this point is located closer to the centroid.

2.5. Contribution of Dimensions to Points or Squared Correlations

The next step in interpreting the results is to decide how well each point is described by each dimension. This is expressed by the contributions of dimensions to points, which provide information on how much of the inertia of a point is explained by a dimension. These contributions are calculated using the formula

$$cr_i = \frac{f_i^2}{d_i^2} = \cos^2\omega \tag{2.8}$$

The contribution of dimensions to points is independent of the mass of the point and it indicates how well the point is described by the dimension concerned. These contributions are often called *squared correlations*, since they are the same as $\cos^2$ for the angle between the line from the centroid to the point and the principal axes. Hereafter the term squared correlation will be used to avoid confusion with the contribution of the points to dimensions. If *cr* for a dimension is high, the angle between the vector of the point and the axis is small. The point is therefore situated in the direction of the axis, which implies a high correlation with the dimension (see Figure 2.3).

The sum of the *cr* values for each profile point over *all dimensions* (two in our example) is equal to 1.0. When analyzing larger tables, however, only a small number of dimensions are of interest. In such cases, the sum of the squared correlations expresses the goodness of fit of each point's representation in the solution, and is often termed the *quality* of the description of each point. This statistic is equivalent to communalities in principal component analysis.

Table 2.5 shows the squared correlations for our example. We see that the first dimension explains 100% of the inertia for the Oslo area and 91% for north Norway. For mid Norway the corresponding

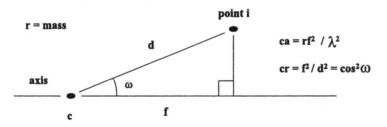

Figure 2.3. Illustration of the Calculation of the Contribution of Points to the Inertia of Each Dimension and the Squared Correlations

share is 59%. The second dimension explains 41% of the inertia for mid Norway, only 9% for north Norway, and 0% for Oslo.

Similarly it can be seen that all the crimes are explained relatively well by the first dimension. This applies to fraud in particular, which is explained by as much as 99%. The second dimension explains 29% of the burglaries and 23% of the crimes of vandalism.

It is essential to understand the difference between the two kinds of contributions. *The contributions of points to dimensions serve primarily as guides to the interpretation of the dimensions, whereas the squared correlations indicate how well a point is described by the dimension.* Usually, high contributions of points to dimensions will imply high squared correlations, but not the reverse (Greenacre, 1984). Because both of these statistics are always positive, it is important to inspect the coordinates to see in what direction on a dimension a point is located.

2.6. The Interdependence of the Points

Distances and coordinates are calculated separately within each set of points, and the solutions are presented in a common or joint space. This can be done because the two sets of points are related or interdependent, hence the name "correspondence analysis." The sets of points are related in the following ways:

1. The space for the rows and the space for the columns have the same dimensionality.
2. Eigenvalues are the same for the two solutions.
3. The coordinates of the row points can be calculated on the basis of the row profiles and the coordinates of the column points, and vice versa for the other set of points. The relationships can be formulated as

$$r_i = \frac{\Sigma_j\big((ar_{ij})(c_j)\big)}{\lambda} \qquad (2.9a)$$

$$c_j = \frac{\Sigma_i\big((ac_{ij})(r_i)\big)}{\lambda} \qquad (2.9b)$$

where r_i and c_j are row coordinates and column coordinates, ar_{ij} and ac_{ij} are elements in the row and the column profiles, and λ is the square root of the dimension's eigenvalue (i.e., the singular value).

Equations 2.9a and 2.9b are called transition formulas and they describe how to move from one coordinate matrix to the other. These equations also show that a specific row profile attracts the column categories that are the most dominating in the row profile concerned.

The configuration of a particular set of points reflects similarities and differences within this set, whereas the joint configuration indicates correspondence between the two sets of points. This distinction implies that distances between the points are defined only within each set of points, whereas distances between points from different sets are not defined explicitly. However, it is legitimate to interpret a point's relative position in relation to *all* the points in the other set.

Another important property is the so-called *principle of distributional equivalence*. This implies that if two profiles are identical, they can be combined into one category without affecting the result for the other set of points. In the case of very large tables it may often be expedient to combine categories having almost similar profiles, thus making it easier to interpret the results. This stability in distances is a unique property of the chi-square metric.

2.7. Supplementary Points

A very useful property of correspondence analysis is the possibility of using supplementary information as an aid in interpreting the results. Let us illustrate this by means of our data example in Table 2.1. This table contains some categories that have not been used as yet in the analysis. First of all, the total distribution of crimes over the whole country is shown in the bottom row. Second, the last two columns show the distributions of people living in different regions for sparsely populated and densely populated areas, obtained from a nationwide survey in Norway. Using the transition formulas, these categories can be projected into our configuration without affecting the solution.

Figure 2.4 shows the configuration of *active* and *supplementary* points. The active points, in our case parts of the country and crimes, contribute to the total inertia and the position of the dimensions. The supplementary points, on the other hand, can be regarded as points without mass, and their relative positions provide additional information as regards interpreting the configuration.

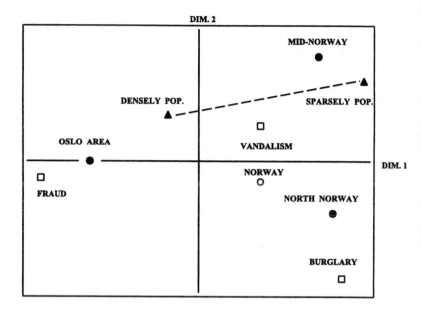

Figure 2.4. Graphic Presentation of the Results of Correspondence Analysis Applied to Table 2.1 with Supplementary Points

The supplementary points do not contribute to the inertia of the dimensions. We can, however, calculate the squared correlations for these points, and these express how well a point is described by each dimension.

If we examine the configuration we see that the point that represents the whole country lies in the direction of mid Norway and north Norway. This means that these two parts of the country have profiles relatively similar to the profile for the country as a whole, whereas Oslo is more atypical.

The other two supplementary points belong to the other set of points. We note that "sparsely populated" lies in the direction of vandalism and burglary, whereas "densely populated" lies closer to fraud. That sparsely populated tends toward north Norway and mid Norway, and densely populated toward Oslo is immediately meaningful, since Oslo is the capital city of Norway.

Table 2.5 (on page 18) shows the squared correlations of the supplementary points. We see that the whole country is well described by dimension 1. As far as sparsely populated versus densely populated is concerned, the former is well described by dimension 1 (89%), whereas the latter is best described by dimension 2 (82%).

In a further analysis it would be natural to include more parts of the country and more types of crimes, which could contribute to new dimensions and allow more detailed interpretation of results. Including supplementary points in a correspondence analysis also makes it possible to check the validity of the results. Since these points do not influence the solution to the active elements, they serve as external criteria.

Outliers

Extreme profiles, or outliers, are often a problem in correspondence analysis. If one profile point deviates to a very large degree from the others in the set, this point will often have a dominating effect on the results of the analysis. This occurs when the point both makes a large absolute contribution and also has a high coordinate value to an axis (Hoffman and Franke, 1986). This often leads to the outlier occupying a position far distance from the other points, which are thus pressed closer together.

This problem can be solved by treating the outlier as a supplementary point, in which case it does not contribute to the formation of the dimensions. This makes it possible to undertake a more detailed and precise interpretation of the structure seen in relation to the rest of the points.

2.8. Interpretation and Dimensionality

The interpretation of the configuration of the points is based on the chi-square distances between points, and these distances are defined separately for each set of points. This implies that if two row points lie close together, the profiles of these two points are similar. As the profiles become more dissimilar, so the points become further apart; the same condition applies to the relation between the column points. The marginal profiles for both sets of points lie on the origin of the axes, so that a point with a profile like the average will also lie in this center. It is important to recognize, however, that two points positioned close together in a low-dimensional solution may lie far apart in a solution with higher dimensionality.

As far as the distances between row points and column points is concerned, the relation is more complicated since these distances are not defined as chi-square distances. All the points in one set of points contribute to determine the position of every point in the other set of points, and vice versa. This means that caution must be exercised when interpreting the distance between two points from different sets of points. Usually, however, the points i and j will be close to each other when $f(ij) > e(ij)$, and the distance will be great when $f(ij) < e(ij)$, where $f(ij)$ is the observed and $e(ij)$ is the expected frequency (van der Heijden, 1987). In our example this means that the cells representing "Oslo/fraud," "mid Norway/vandalism," and "north Norway/burglary" include more observations than expected on the basis of the marginal distributions. Carroll, Green, and Schaffer (1986, 1987), however, proposed a procedure that makes it possible to compare distances both within and between sets of points.

In addition to the proximity of the points and their constellations in space, it is usual practice to interpret the dimensions and give them a name by studying the distribution of the points and their order along the dimensions. This corresponds to the interpretation of the results in, for example, factor analysis and multidimensional scaling. The contribution of points to the dimensions supplies additional information about which points are most important for the dimension.

How many dimensions should one try to interpret? A general rule is to keep the number of dimensions as low as possible. In other words, it is best to try to explain the data by means of the fewest possible parameters (the principle of scientific parsimony). On the other hand, the solution should describe the data as fully as possible, implying that the percentage share of explained inertia should be high. Thus the solution to the problem of dimensionality implies weighing a high percentage inertia, on the one hand, against low dimensionality, on the other. Several criteria can be applied to solve this problem:

The Scree Test ("The Elbow Criterion")

If the eigenvalues are plotted by increasing dimensionality, the result is a falling curve. If this curve, after a relatively steep downward trend, flattens out, this indicates that the right dimensionality is equal to the point where the curve shows a bend ("an elbow"). The scree test was proposed by Cattell (1966) for use within the context of factor analysis.

Interpretability

If the dimensions can be interpreted in a sensible manner, this indicates that they are justified. If one comes across a dimension that cannot be interpreted, this could indicate that it is just a result of random fluctuations among the residuals.

Reproducibility

If it is possible to obtain a parallel set of data, for example, subgroups from the same population, analyses of the two sets of data should give concordant results. If the solutions give n corresponding dimensions, this indicates that the correct dimensionality is n.

2.9. Assumptions and Restrictions

In Chapter 1 it was mentioned that correspondence analysis often is described as a model-free method, and that few restrictions and assumptions are made. It *is* basically an exploratory and descriptive technique, which uncovers and describes the associations in large contingency tables. The only restriction is that the data elements must be nonnegative numbers (Greenacre as cited in Nishisato, 1980). There are no further assumptions regarding the distribution or the nature of the data.

Nevertheless, some authors prefer not to label correspondence analysis as a model-free method (van der Heijden, Mooijaart, and Takane, 1994), because by choosing the method certain aspects of the data are emphasized. By applying correspondence analysis, we actually choose to focus on the association between the variables and we choose the chi-square metric for the geometrical space. However, the main point for the applied scientist is that the method can be employed to describe graphically almost any contingency table on the assumption that there exists an association to be described. Furthermore, the contingency table ought to be relatively large.

This chapter has introduced the basic concepts of correspondence analysis and, hopefully, supplied the reader with the necessary background to apply the method and to interpret its results. The next chapter will present analyses of larger tables, and thus demonstrate more clearly the advantages of the technique.

3. ANALYSIS OF LARGE TABLES

3.1. Tables with Two Variables

Let us now consider an analysis of a large two-way contingency table. The data are taken from the 1985 health survey in Norway (Statistics Norway, 1987). The main purpose of this survey was to obtain comprehensive knowledge of health problems in the Norwegian population. A total of 10,576 persons were interviewed, with a response rate of 78%. The data are shown in Table 3.1, and presented in a two-way contingency table with two polytomous variables: age (6 groups) and disease at time of interview (12 groups).

Table 3.2 shows the decomposed eigenvalues for the total solution in five dimensions. According to the "elbow criterion," it is natural to choose the two-dimensional solution, which explains as much as 97.4% of the total inertia. It should also be noted that the first dimension is very dominant, accounting for 82.9% of the total inertia.

The two-dimensional solution for both sets of points is shown graphically in Figure 3.1. The figure shows that the age groups are ranked by falling age along the first dimension. The configuration

TABLE 3.1

Number of Cases of the Various Diseases at Time of Interview in Different Age Groups (per 1000)

Type of Disease		0–6	7–15	16–24	25–44	45–66	67+	Tot.
Nervous disorders	NERDIS	12	22	35	68	102	147	386
Nervous system	NERSYS	7	11	35	45	49	33	180
Eye and ear	EYEEAR	44	47	45	42	68	155	401
Cardiovascular	CARVAS	12	6	5	38	222	469	752
Respiratory organs	RESPIR	63	70	69	74	80	84	440
Stomach ulcer	ULCER	0	1	8	14	36	37	96
Other digestive dis.	DIGEST	9	5	5	15	32	64	130
Urinary/genital system	URIGEN	8	9	30	28	39	56	170
Skin and subcutis	SKIN	103	110	138	124	88	54	617
Musculoskeletal dis.	MUSCSK	22	43	105	165	314	334	983
Other diseases	OTHER	30	42	42	72	126	235	547
Injuries	INJUR	7	13	38	32	48	76	214
Total		317	379	555	717	1204	1744	4916

Age Groups are shown across the columns 0–6, 7–15, 16–24, 25–44, 45–66, 67+.

TABLE 3.2

Eigenvalues, Percentage Explained Inertia, and Histogram

	Eigenvalues	Percent	
1.	0.19140	82.94	***
2.	0.03344	14.49	******* Sum 97.43%
3.	0.00391	1.69	*
4.	0.00147	0.64	*
5.	0.00056	0.24	*

Sum eigenvalues: 0.23078; $\chi^2 = 0.23078 \times 4916 = 1134.5$; df = 55

further shows that points representing children (0–15 years) and young adults (16–44 years) form two clusters. For the four youngest age groups the coordinates on dimension 1 are positive; for the older age groups they are negative.

The relative positions of the two sets of points give a picture of which diseases and which age groups are related. Eye and ear

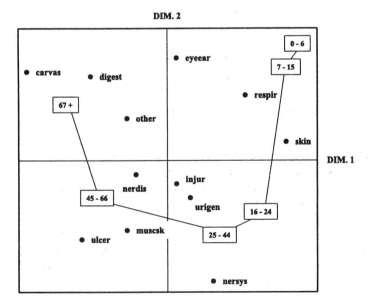

Figure 3.1. Correspondence Analysis of Data from Table 3.1, Showing the Graphical Display of Dimensions 1 and 2

diseases (EYEEAR), respiratory disorders (RESPIR), and skin diseases (SKIN) are relatively more frequent among the youngest, and cardiovascular diseases (CARVAS) and digestive disorders (DIGEST) dominate among the oldest.

The figure further shows that the age group 45-66 years is positioned close to disorders such as stomach ulcer (ULCER), nervous disorders (NERDIS), and musculoskeletal complaints (MUSCSK). It seems reasonable to interpret dimension 1 as an age-specific disease dimension.

As for the second dimension, we may discern a typical phenomenon that occurs quite frequently in connection with both correspondence analysis and multidimensional scaling, namely, the so-called *horseshoe* or *Guttman effect*. This effect often occurs when the first dimension is very dominating, and dimension 2 then becomes a quadratic transformation of dimension 1. Many statisticians have tried to explain this phenomenon and the effect is discussed in detail in van Rijckesvorsel (1987).

The configuration shows, however, that the point representing eye and ear disorders (EYEEAR) loads high on dimension 2, together with children and the elderly. This is the only type of disease with relatively more cases in both these age groups. This suggests that the horseshoe pattern does not exist here as an artifact, but that it is caused by the fact that eye and ear diseases are relatively more predominant in both the very young and the very old.

Table 3.3 shows descriptive statistics for both sets of points. The first column shows the masses of the points and the second their distance from the centroid. Masses with high values show, first, which age groups are associated with most cases of disease and, second, which disease groups (types) include most cases. The masses are a measure of the importance of the point profile in the analysis. The distances, on the other hand, show the degree to which the profile of the point deviates from the average profile. The results show that the profiles get closer and closer to the average with increasing age, except in the oldest age group. As far as disease type is concerned, it can be seen, for example, that skin diseases (SKIN) and cardiovascular disorders (CARVAS) are the types with the most deviating profiles.

If we examine the contributions of the points to dimension 1, it will be seen that in the case of the age variable, the young and the old contribute most to this dimension. For the diseases, three types of

TABLE 3.3

Descriptive Statistics for Columns (Age Groups) and Rows
(Type of Disease)

Name	Masses	Dist.	Coordinates		CONTR		CORR2		Quality
			F1	F2	F1	F2	F1	F2	F1 + F2
0-6	0.064	0.72	0.76	0.38	0.19	0.28	0.79	0.20	0.99
7-15	0.077	0.53	0.69	0.22	0.19	0.11	0.90	0.09	0.99
16-24	0.113	0.34	0.54	-0.17	0.17	0.09	0.86	0.08	0.94
25-44	0.146	0.12	0.26	-0.22	0.05	0.21	0.55	0.40	0.95
45-66	0.245	0.07	-0.21	-0.14	0.05	0.15	0.62	0.29	0.91
67+	0.355	0.20	-0.43	0.12	0.34	0.16	0.92	0.08	1.00
NERDIS	0.079	0.04	-0.13	-0.11	0.01	0.03	0.49	0.31	0.80
NERSYS	0.037	0.23	0.25	-0.41	0.01	0.18	0.26	0.72	0.98
EYEEAR	0.082	0.09	0.12	0.27	0.01	0.18	0.16	0.82	0.98
CARVAS	0.153	0.47	-0.67	0.17	0.36	0.14	0.94	0.06	1.00
RESPIR	0.090	0.30	0.52	0.13	0.13	0.05	0.92	0.06	0.98
ULCER	0.020	0.20	-0.34	-0.27	0.01	0.04	0.59	0.35	0.94
DIGEST	0.026	0.13	-0.30	0.16	0.01	0.02	0.69	0.20	0.89
URIGEN	0.035	0.05	0.05	-0.15	0.00	0.02	0.05	0.43	0.48
SKIN	0.126	0.67	0.82	0.06	0.44	0.02	0.99	0.01	1.00
MUSCSK	0.200	0.07	-0.14	-0.22	0.02	0.28	0.29	0.67	0.96
OTHER	0.111	0.03	-0.14	0.09	0.01	0.03	0.60	0.27	0.87
INJUR	0.044	0.06	0.01	-0.13	0.00	0.02	0.00	0.30	0.30

diseases stand out, namely, skin diseases (SKIN), respiratory disorders (RESPIR), and cardiovascular diseases (CARVAS) (total 91.9% of the inertia of dimension 1). In the case of dimension 2, however, it is seen that the contributions of the different age groups are more evenly distributed, but three types of diseases especially have contributed to the creation of this dimension: musculoskeletal disorders (MUSCSK), diseases of the nervous system (NERSYS), and eye/ear diseases (EYEEAR). The configuration shows that we have a dimension consisting of diseases that are typical in children and the elderly rather than in the middle aged.

The next two columns show the squared correlations that express how large a share of the inertia of the point each of the dimensions explains. The sum of these figures, for each category, represents the quality of description of each point. In the case of this two-dimensional solution, there are only two points for which relatively little of the variance is explained, namely, urinary/genital (URIGEN) disorders (48%) and injuries (INJUR) (30%). These points lie outside the plane and are inaccurately described. All the other points in both sets are very well described in the two-dimensional solution.

3.2. Tables with More Than Two Variables

So far we have only considered correspondence analysis of two-way contingency tables, but it is also possible to analyze multivariate tables. This can be done in several ways, and we shall consider one of the most usual methods.

Table 3.4 shows a three-way classification of the variables disease (D), age (A), and sex (S), which gives a $12 \times 6 \times 2$ matrix, with a total of 144 cells. One way to analyze this table is to transform it into a two-way matrix by combining two variables into one "interactive variable," or rather, we treat two of the variables as one variable. In the case of Table 3.4 it is possible to create three tables: $D \times (A \times S)$, $A \times (D \times S)$, and $S \times (D \times A)$, where the interactive variable is shown in brackets. Within the French tradition these kinds of tables are called *multiple tables*, and are very commonly used in the study of multivariate contingency tables.

The choice of which table to analyze is very important since the interaction between the two variables making up the interactive variable will *not* affect the result of the analysis. For this reason it is best to combine the two variables that constitute the interaction of least interest. In the foregoing case, the interaction between age and sex is of least interest since what is of primary interest is the relation of each of these variables to disease. Thus, the "new" two-way table consists of the variable *type of disease* (12 categories) and *sex combined with age* (12 categories).

As Table 3.5 shows, the analysis gives a total of 11 dimensions, of which the first 3 explain 94.6% of the total inertia. Let us tentatively choose the three-dimensional solution on the basis of the elbow criterion: the eigenvalues of the dimensions are 0.190, 0.037, and 0.018. The singular values (0.436, 0.192, and 0.134) can be interpreted as maximal canonical correlations between the independent variables (age and sex) and the dependent variable (disease) (van der Heijden and de Leeuw, 1985).

Figure 3.2 is a graphic presentation of the results for the first two dimensions and shows that the configuration is very much the same

TABLE 3.4
Three-Way Classification of the Variables Disease, Age, and Sex (per 1000)

| | Age Groups | | | | | | | | | | | |
| | Men | | | | | | Women | | | | | |
Disease	0-6	7-15	16-24	25-44	45-67	67+	0-6	7-15	16-24	25-44	45-66	67+
NERDIS	8	25	23	46	66	106	17	19	45	89	135	179
NERSYS	4	13	30	29	29	31	10	9	41	60	68	34
EYEEAR	38	52	41	48	72	156	50	44	48	36	64	155
CARVAS	10	7	5	39	226	399	15	5	5	38	218	523
RESPIR	70	77	72	77	89	100	56	64	67	70	72	72
ULCER	0	0	8	22	43	43	0	3	8	5	29	33
DIGEST	12	3	3	16	21	60	6	6	6	15	42	68
URIGEN	10	11	11	12	22	72	6	8	48	45	55	43
SKIN	105	106	119	106	72	55	100	113	156	141	104	54
MUSCSK	12	36	95	153	267	266	33	49	115	177	358	387
OTHER	38	47	41	52	101	192	21	37	44	92	150	268
INJUR	4	13	55	46	63	77	10	14	23	19	34	74

TABLE 3.5

Eigenvalues, Percentage Explained Inertia, and Histogram

	Eigenvalue	*Percent*	
1	0.18973	73.34	***********************************
2	0.03690	14.26	*******
3	0.01799	6.95	***
4	0.00595	2.30	*
5	0.00373	1.44	*
6	0.00194	0.75	*
7	0.00107	0.41	*
8	0.00093	0.36	*
9	0.00036	0.14	*
10	0.00009	0.03	*
11	0.00000	0.00	*

Sum: 0.25869; $\chi^2 = (0.25869) \times 9785 = \underline{2531.3}$; df = 121

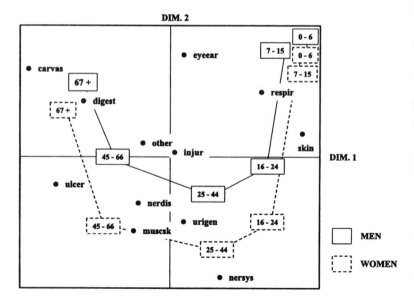

Figure 3.2. Correspondence Analysis of Data from Table 3.4, Showing the Display of Dimensions 1 and 2

as in Figure 3.1. The first dimension shows the relative differences in prevalence of disease among the different age groups, whereas dimension 2 shows, among other things, differences between the sexes. It can be seen from the figure that the difference by sex is most marked in the age groups from 16 to 66 years. This implies that diseases of the nervous system, urinary/genital diseases, musculoskeletal disorders, and nervous disorders are relatively more prevalent among women than among men aged 16–66 years, and relatively more prevalent among the middle aged than among the young and the elderly.

Figure 3.3 shows the second and third dimensions. A striking feature of this configuration is the three clusterings that appear. Two of these clusterings are made up of adult men versus adult women, which load on each end of dimension 3. The most marked feature is that men between 16 and 66 are placed close to stomach ulcers and injuries, whereas the corresponding group of females is grouped together with nervous disorders and urinary/genital diseases. All in

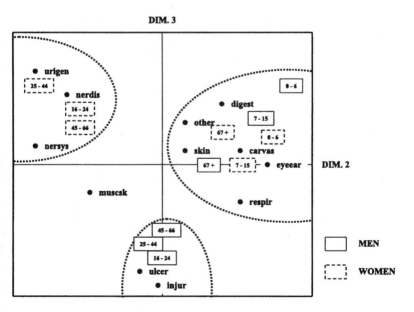

Figure 3.3. Graphical Display of Dimensions 2 and 3 Based on Data from Table 3.4

all, the configuration of the two sets of points in all three dimensions seems to be meaningful and agrees with the existing knowledge about the relationship between sex, age, and disease. Table 3.6 shows the descriptive statistics of this analysis, and the results will be briefly discussed.

Masses

The masses are seen to increase with age for both sexes. This means that the number of cases of disease increases with increasing age. As far as the disease types are concerned, most cases are found within the categories musculoskeletal disorders, cardiovascular diseases, and skin (cutis and subcutis) diseases, with the fewest cases in the categories stomach ulcers, other digestive disorders, and diseases of the urinary/genital systems.

Distances

The second column in Table 3.6 gives the distance of the points from the centroid. A profile that is very different from the average profile is thus represented by a point far from this center. We note that the values are highest for the youngest group, and that, of the diseases, the points for skin diseases, cardiovascular diseases, stomach ulcer, and other diseases are farthest away.

Coordinates

These show the position of the points in space, which have already been examined in Figures 3.2 and 3.3.

Contributions of Points to the Inertia of Dimensions

Dimension 1. The table shows that the points skin diseases, cardiovascular disorders, and diseases in respiratory organs contribute as much as 92% to the inertia of the first dimension. In the case of the column profiles (age and sex), the greatest contributions are made by the youngest and the oldest groups, and this applies to both sexes. The graphical display reveals that the young show relatively many cases of skin (cutis/subcutis) diseases and of respiratory disorders, whereas cardiovascular diseases are most frequent among the elderly.

Dimension 2. This dimension is dominated by the points musculoskeletal complaints, diseases of the nervous system, and eye/ear

TABLE 3.6

Descriptive Statistics for Columns (Sex and Age) and Rows
(Type of Disease)

Name	Mass	Dist.	Coordinates			CONTR			CORR2			Qual
			F1	F2	F3	F1	F2	F3	F1	F2	F3	
Men												
0–6	0.032	0.90	0.80	0.44	0.17	0.11	0.17	0.05	0.72	0.21	0.03	0.96
7–15	0.040	0.54	0.68	0.24	0.08	0.10	0.06	0.01	0.85	0.10	0.01	0.96
16–24	0.051	0.41	0.54	−0.07	−0.30	0.08	0.01	0.26	0.70	0.01	0.22	0.93
25–44	0.066	0.13	0.24	−0.11	−0.22	0.02	0.02	0.19	0.43	0.10	0.39	0.92
45–66	0.109	0.11	−0.24	−0.01	−0.20	0.03	0.00	0.25	0.52	0.00	0.38	0.90
67+	0.159	0.17	−0.37	0.15	0.01	0.11	0.10	0.00	0.77	0.13	0.00	0.90
Sum						0.45	0.36	0.75				
Women												
0–6	0.033	0.59	0.69	0.29	0.04	0.08	0.08	0.00	0.80	0.14	0.00	0.94
7–15	0.038	0.52	0.69	0.19	0.00	0.10	0.04	0.00	0.91	0.07	0.00	0.98
16–24	0.062	0.39	0.54	−0.22	0.09	0.10	0.08	0.03	0.77	0.12	0.02	0.91
25–44	0.080	0.21	0.27	−0.32	0.18	0.03	0.22	0.14	0.35	0.49	0.15	0.99
45–66	0.136	0.10	−0.19	−0.23	0.07	0.03	0.19	0.04	0.36	0.54	0.05	0.95
67+	0.193	0.24	−0.47	0.09	0.06	0.22	0.05	0.04	0.92	0.04	0.02	0.98
Sum						0.55	0.64	0.25				
NERDIS	0.077	0.08	−0.13	−0.18	0.14	0.01	0.07	0.09	0.22	0.39	0.26	0.87
NERSYS	0.037	0.29	0.25	−0.46	0.05	0.01	0.21	0.00	0.22	0.73	0.01	0.96
EYEEAR	0.082	0.11	0.12	0.29	0.01	0.01	0.18	0.00	0.13	0.77	0.00	0.90
CARVAS	0.152	0.48	−0.67	0.18	0.02	0.36	0.13	0.00	0.93	0.06	0.00	0.99
RESPIR	0.091	0.31	0.51	0.18	−0.07	0.13	0.08	0.02	0.85	0.11	0.01	0.97
ULCER	0.020	0.34	−0.35	−0.09	−0.38	0.01	0.00	0.16	0.36	0.02	0.43	0.81
DIGEST	0.026	0.17	−0.30	0.13	0.13	0.01	0.01	0.03	0.54	0.10	0.10	0.74
URIGEN	0.035	0.23	0.07	−0.22	0.26	0.00	0.05	0.13	0.02	0.21	0.28	0.51
SKIN	0.126	0.66	0.81	0.05	0.04	0.43	0.01	0.01	0.99	0.00	0.00	0.99
MUSCSK	0.199	0.08	−0.14	−0.22	−0.07	0.02	0.25	0.05	0.27	0.61	0.06	0.94
OTHER	0.111	0.04	−0.13	0.06	0.10	0.01	0.01	0.07	0.41	0.08	0.26	0.75
INJUR	0.044	0.22	0.01	0.00	−0.42	0.00	0.00	0.44	0.00	0.00	0.82	0.82

diseases, and these points explain 64% of the inertia of this dimension. As far as the other set of points is concerned, it is seen that women dominate this factor (64% of the inertia). If the contributions of points to dimensions are compared with the configuration, it is seen that the youngest age groups experience relatively more eye/ear diseases, while musculoskeletal disorders, nervous system disorders, and nervous disorders are most prevalent among women.

Dimension 3. Looking at the third factor, it is seen that this is explained mainly by the points injuries, stomach ulcer, and diseases of the urinary system (73%). Note as well that this factor is dominated by men, which explains as much as 75% of the inertia of the dimension. If we examine the configuration as well, we find that injuries and stomach ulcer are related to men aged 16 to 66 years, and that diseases of the urinary system and genitals are related in particular to women aged 25 to 44 years. These results indicate that we have discovered an interaction between the three variables, that is, that the relationships between disease type and age are different in men and women, respectively.

Squared Correlations

If we examine the squared correlations we see that they follow the same pattern as the absolute contributions. This means that the points that define the different dimensions are also described best by the respective dimensions. If we look at the sum of the relative contributions for this solution (the "quality" of the descriptions of the points), we see that nearly all the points are described well. The least well described are urinary/genital diseases (51%), other digestive disorders (74%), and other diseases (75%).

This analysis has provided a simple picture of the structure of our data matrix. The graphical display shows in a lucid way how the variables sex, age, and disease are related. One of the greatest benefits achieved with this type of analysis is that it makes communication of complex relations much easier. The benefit increases as the size of the table increases.

4. ANALYSIS OF MULTIPLE RESPONSE TABLES AND SURVEY DATA

4.1. Bourdieu's Concept of Social Space

Correspondence analysis can be a very useful method to describe and visualize relationships between several variables and categories in survey data. One of the most famous applications of such analyses was presented by the French sociologist Pierre Bourdieu in his book *Distinction* (1984). There he presented an analysis of a large quantity of survey material on consumption and preferences among different socio-occupational groups in France. With the help of correspondence analysis, he explored and visualized what he denotes as a social space. The different occupational types and the different preferences are depicted in a joint three-dimensional geometrical space. The first two dimensions are defined by volume of capital and composition of capital, whereas the third dimension constitutes changes in these two properties over time. The term "capital" is used to mean the overall set of resources and powers the individuals possess, including economic, cultural, and social capital (Bourdieu, 1984). This chapter presents a similar application of correspondence analysis, but on a much smaller scale.

4.2. Data to Be Analyzed

The data matrix to be analyzed is presented in Table 4.1. This table is a multiresponse table composed of several separate cross-classifications and conditional distributions that are concatenated into one table. The data derive from a survey of social assistance recipients in Norway. According to a classification analysis these clients were classified into four distinct subgroups: the *sick*, the *deviants*, the *dependents*, and the *indebted* (Clausen, 1996).

The *sick* were characterized by poor health, both mentally and physically, and by extensive use of sedatives. Most of the *deviants* had been convicted of a crime, had a relatively high consumption of alcohol, and many had used narcotics. The third group, called the *dependents*, reported severe difficulties in meeting daily expenses and had received social assistance for a long period. Most of them had been unemployed for several years. The last group was labeled the

TABLE 4.1

The Raw Data Matrix for Correspondence Analysis

Variables	Sick	Deviants	Dependents	Indebted
Classification variables				
Poor mental health	139	40	40	41
Poor general health	132	42	37	53
Using sedatives	131	21	16	15
National insurance	124	51	64	124
Low education	101	45	49	62
Alcohol consumption	15	79	5	4
Convicted	20	98	34	29
Alcohol problems	24	47	1	2
Ever used narcotics	5	42	10	1
Debts due to penalty	7	65	12	6
Daily cigarette smoking	137	114	106	159
Long-term client	61	67	115	62
Trouble daily expenses	95	44	83	86
Trouble NOK2000	143	83	121	149
Unemployed	57	97	92	98
House debt	76	32	56	195
Owns a dwelling	75	49	43	194
Owns a car	63	45	38	171
"High" income	48	46	18	143
Other variables				
Men	49	113	46	105
Women	111	11	76	95
Age 18–24	21	38	23	34
Age 25–30	24	36	33	60
Age 30–50	115	50	66	106
Unmarried	64	90	66	69
Married	24	8	15	72
Divorced	71	26	40	58
Rural	57	32	29	82
Urban	72	53	55	65
City	30	37	37	52
Child not in household	25	44	18	28
Child in household	86	15	66	149

indebted, and most of them had relatively high housing debts. Rather than being directly poor, these clients had high levels of expenses that exceeded their incomes.

To elaborate the classification analysis further, we want to relate the client typology and the variables that formed the basis of the classification, and add demographic variables that did not enter into the classification procedure. In this way we want to visualize a kind of social space for the clients by displaying the client types in a joint space with behaviors and background characteristics. The analysis is partly a visualization of the earlier classification and partly adds new information to this analysis by entering new variables to refine the previous results. In addition, the demographic variables will serve as a validity check of the classification. We may consider the client types as the dependent variable (the variable to be described) and all the others as independent or describing variables. The analysis presented here is strictly descriptive and serves primarily illustrative purposes. It must be pointed out that the chi-square test is not applicable to this multiple response table.

4.3. Results: A Social Space of Welfare Clients

Figure 4.1 shows the geometrical display of the first two dimensions, as determined by the correspondence analysis. The two-dimensional solution explains 86.8% of the total inertia. The contributions of points to the dimensions and the squared correlations will not be presented in this section, but the reader may refer to Appendix C, where the SPSS commands and results are reproduced.

The configuration reveals three separate clusterings that represent the deviants, the sick, and the indebted. The first (horizontal) dimension refers primarily to deviant behaviors. Both conviction and drug use load high on this first dimension. By projecting the demographical variables on the axis, it is shown that young, unmarried men living in cities are closest to the deviants. This strongly corroborates with our knowledge about the background characteristics of deviant or criminal populations.

On the second dimension, the indebted and the sick load high on each end of the dimension. It is the middle-aged divorced women that lie in the direction of the sick, whereas the young adult married men are located among the indebted. These results are in accordance

40

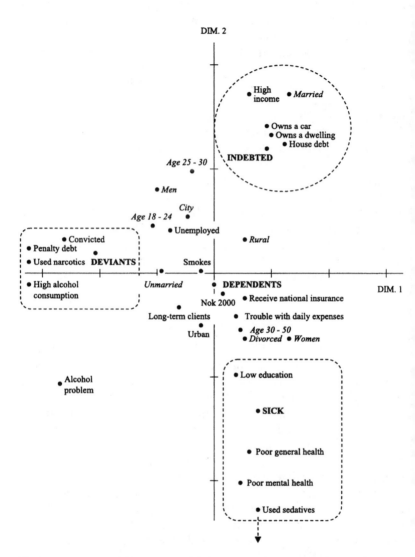

Figure 4.1. A Social Space of Social Assistance Recipients. Correspondence Analysis of Data in Table 4.1 (the Demographic Variables Are Printed in Italics)

with the knowledge we have about social assistance recipients in Norway.

The last group, termed the dependents, is situated near the centroid and is poorly described in this two-dimensional solution. To describe these clients properly we would have to analyze the data in three dimensions.

Appendix C gives the qualities of the description of each point in the two-dimensional solution (the column "Total" in the tables labeled Contribution of dimensions to the inertia of each row/column point). These values show that the following points are poorly described: daily cigarette smoking, trouble daily expenses, trouble NOK2000, unemployed, long-term client, and dependents. Since type of client has four categories, these points will be perfectly described in the three-dimensional solution, and these points define the third dimension.

This analysis illustrates one way to apply correspondence analysis to survey data. A natural extension would be to add more independent or describing variables (row variables), which would produce a more complex display and describe the clients in more detail.

Screening Data

Correspondence analysis may be used to screen survey data by examining the relations among a large set of variables. Suppose a researcher is in the initial phase of data processing and analysis, and the primary interest is to describe different socio-occupational groups. In this situation, correspondence analysis might be rather useful.

First cross-tabulate the variable socio-occupational groups against a large set of relevant variables, and concatenate these tables into one multiple response table. This might be done in SPSS by the procedure MULT RESPONSE. Then, analyze this table by correspondence analysis, which will supply the researcher with a map of the relations among the different variable categories. This map may be very helpful as a guide for further analyses of the data. To be able to see these numerous relations in a single glance is one of the greatest heuristic advantages of correspondence analysis. Additionally, studying Bourdieu's presentation of social space can help in further understanding the potential of this analysis method.

Finally, the SPSS version of correspondence analysis (ANACOR), with which the present author is most familiar, contains some weaknesses when applied to these kinds of data. First, there is no interface between the subprograms MULT RESPONSE and ANA-COR. This implies that analyzing very large matrices will involve a rather cumbersome job setup procedure (cf. Appendix C). Second, there is no option in ANACOR to use supplementary information. Since this property is very useful, both as regards interpreting a configuration and applied to outliers, it is highly desirable that this option become available in later versions of the program.

5. CORRESPONDENCE ANALYSIS
AND LOGLINEAR MODELS

In Anglo-American social science, the loglinear model is one of the most widely used methods for analyzing categorical variables. It is a very powerful method for analyses of multivariate contingency tables, especially for uncovering interactions between variables. Correspondence analysis and loglinear models have different advantages, so the choice of method depends on the type of data to be analyzed and on what relations or effects are of most interest. In the following sections the reader is presumed to have some knowledge of loglinear models. An elementary and adequate introduction to the method is to be found in Knoke and Burke (1980).

Considering the current increasing interest in correspondence analysis, it is natural to consider the relationship between the two methods. This issue is discussed in detail in, for example, Goodman (1987) and van der Heijden and de Leeuw (1985), but in different contexts. In this chapter the two methods of analysis will be compared and it will be shown how they can be used to supplement each other. The presentation is largely based on van der Heijden and de Leeuw's instructive article on the same subject.

The following is a general rule for deciding when each method is to be preferred: correspondence analysis is very suitable for discovering the inherent structure of contingency tables with variables containing a large number of categories. Loglinear models are particularly suitable for analyzing multivariate contingency tables, where the variables contain relatively few categories. Loglinear models analyze mainly the interrelationships between a set of variables, whereas correspondence analysis examines the relations between the categories of the variables.

Correspondence analysis can be regarded as a method for decomposing the difference in chi-square values between two specific loglinear models. In the most usual cases, that is, when operating with two-way frequency tables, the analysis consists of decomposing the chi-square difference between the independence model [1][2] and the saturated model [12]. This implies that correspondence analysis produces a graphical display of the *association* between the two variables. Consequently, it is advisable to perform a chi-square test before applying correspondence analysis. If the independent model is rejected, then it is legitimate to proceed with correspondence analysis. This does *not* apply to multiple response tables.

5.1. An Example: Analysis of a Three-Way Table

Table 5.1 shows a three-way classification of sex (S), age (A), and alcohol consumption (C). The data were obtained from the nationwide *Survey of Level of Living 1995* in Norway (Statistics Norway, 1996). A total of 3720 persons aged 16 years or more were interviewed, and the response rate amounted to 75.4%. The main purpose of this study was to throw light on the main aspects of the level of living among Norwegians.

The analyses presented in this section will follow the recommendations given by van der Heijden and de Leeuw (1985) for a complementary use of loglinear analysis and correspondence analysis:

1. First carry out a loglinear analysis of the table and use the chi-square statistic to find an acceptable model.

TABLE 5.1

Three-Way Classification of the Variables Age, Sex, and Alcohol Consumption ("How Often Did You Consume Alcohol Last Year?")

	Age Groups					
	16–25	*26–35*	*36–45*	*46–55*	*56–66*	*67–100*
Females						
Many times a week	22	19	83	69	32	22
Once a week	78	84	130	126	62	19
2–3 times a month	109	120	135	99	40	22
Once a month	108	91	108	50	41	29
More seldom	132	203	160	127	95	62
Never	85	90	78	106	126	177
Males						
Many times a week	54	65	105	139	82	39
Once a week	134	127	150	149	63	40
2–3 times a month	114	136	124	103	54	42
Once a month	101	87	67	71	44	36
More seldom	104	81	113	88	84	72
Never	80	35	38	49	53	100

2. Then decide which multiple table to create.

3. Afterward, carry out a correspondence analysis on this matrix.

Loglinear Analysis

Table 5.2 gives the chi-square values for the hierarchical models that have been tested. Two chi-square statistics are presented: the likelihood-ratio chi-square (L^2) and the Pearson chi-square (χ^2). The L^2 statistic has the advantage that it can be partitioned into additive components. It is, however, the Pearson chi-square that forms the basis for the metric in correspondence analysis. It is seen that all the models, except for the saturated one, are rejected. The fact that model M4 is rejected implies that a significant interaction exists between the three variables sex, age, and alcohol consumption. This means that the relation between age and alcohol consumption is different for men and women, respectively, or equivalently, the relationship between sex and alcohol consumption varies according to age.

The estimated parameter values for two and three variable interactions under the saturated model are shown in Table 5.3. The results may be summarized in the following way:

(a) There is a significant association between sex and alcohol consumption. Men drink more often than women.

(b) There is a significant association between age and alcohol consumption. The frequency of drinking increases with age, except for the oldest age group.

TABLE 5.2
Chi-Square Values for Different Models[a]

Model		df	L^2	χ^2	P
Independence	[S][A][C]	60	908.1	976.4	< 0.001
Base	[SA][C]	55	894.6	967.9	< 0.001
M1	[SC][SA]	50	655.8	705.4	< 0.001
M2	[SA][AC]	30	325.7	318.0	< 0.001
M3	[SC][AC]	30	100.3	99.8	< 0.001
M4	[SC][AC][SA]	25	68.5	68.0	< 0.001
Saturated	[SAC]	0	0.0	0.0	1.000

[a]S = sex, A = age, and C = alcohol consumption.

46

Significant Lambda Estimates for the Following Interactions:
[Sex × Alcohol], [Age × Alcohol], and [Sex × Age × Alcohol]

Alcohol Consumption	Sex	Age Groups					
		16–25	26–35	36–45	46–55	56–66	67–100
Two-way interaction							
Many times a week	0.35	−0.52	−0.46	0.31	0.45	0.23	
Once a week	0.14			0.21	0.28		−0.58
2–3 times a month		0.19	0.38	0.18		−0.33	−0.44
Once a month		0.36	0.25		−0.28	−0.18	
More seldom	−0.18				−0.20		
Never	−0.53		−0.40	−0.64	−0.27	0.29	1.09
Three-way interaction							
Many times a week			0.27	−0.13			−0.22
Once a week						−0.16	
2–3 times a month		−0.13					
Once a month					0.19		
More seldom			−0.27	0.11			
Never		0.23					

(c) There is a significant interaction between the three variables sex, age, and alcohol consumption. However, the interpretation of this interaction is not straightforward. It is not easy to see how the association between age and alcohol consumption differs for men and women. It is particularly in this context that correspondence analysis may supplement loglinear analysis and be an aid in the interpretation of the results.

Choice of Multiple Table

Three-way tables and tables of a higher order can be analyzed by means of correspondence analysis by compounding the tables into two-way tables by constructing so-called interactive variables. This was done in the analysis described in Chapter 3. Thus, the first step is to decide which multiple table we want as input to correspondence analysis.

The following guidelines can be applied: First, if one of the variables is considered as a dependent variable, code the independent variables interactively. Second, if there is no dependent variable, construct the interactive variable from the variables that form interactions of least interest. Finally, code the interactive variable from variables that constitute nonsignificant or weak interactions.

In our case, the variable alcohol consumption is considered as a dependent variable, and we are primarily interested in the relationship of this variable to sex and age. This implies the construction of a 6 × 12 multiple table (C × (S × A)), where sex and age are combined to constitute one variable.

Correspondence Analysis

Correspondence analysis of this multiple table implies decomposing the chi-square value of the loglinear model [C][SA] (base model). The results must be interpreted in the light of the difference between the saturated model and [C][SA]. It should be noted that this implies that the interaction [SA] does not influence the result of the analysis. This means that the choice of interactive variable is essential, since this choice will influence the result. If the interaction effect [SAD] had not been significant, we would have to interpret the analysis in the light of the difference between the *base* model and *M4*.

Table 5.4 shows that the correspondence analysis yields five dimensions, of which the first two explain 91.2% of the total inertia. Note that the chi-square value, calculated by multiplying the total inertia by the number of cases, equals the chi-square value for the base model (Table 5.2).

Figure 5.1 presents the graphical display of the two-dimensional solution, and Table 5.5 shows the accompanying descriptive statistics. The first dimension, which explains 67.5% of the total inertia, refers to abstinence versus drinking. The elderly, especially the females, are located near "never consumed any alcohol during the last year." The

TABLE 5.4

Eigenvalues, Percentage Explained Inertia, and Histogram

	Eigenvalues	Percent	
1.	0.10596	67.5	*********************************
2.	0.03726	23.7	************ Sum 91.2%
3.	0.00862	5.5	***
4.	0.00413	2.6	*
5.	0.00111	0.7	*

Sum eigenvalues: 0.15708; $\chi^2 = 0.15708 \times 6162 = 967.9$; df = 55

48

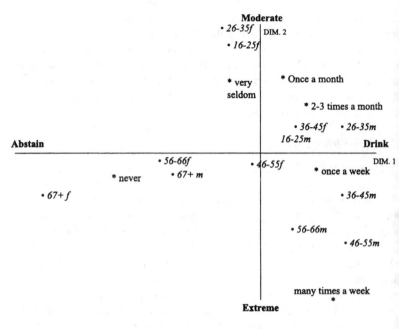

Figure 5.1. Correspondence Analysis of Data in Table 5.1

middle aged, including both men and women, are located at the opposite end of this dimension. The second dimension may be labeled moderate versus extreme drinking patterns. Both "never drinking" and "heavy drinking" are located at the negative end of this dimension, whereas moderate drinking is located at the positive end. By studying the configuration, some interesting features emerge. The young females are relatively more often moderate alcohol consumers, whereas the middle-aged men are inclined to drink most often. It must be pointed out, however, that also this configuration displays a horseshoe-like pattern, similar to the pattern in Figure 3.2.

In this chapter, it has been shown how correspondence analysis and loglinear models can complement each other in a useful way. In contrast to the multitude of effect estimates provided by the loglinear analysis, the correspondence analysis displays a nice graphical representation of the data that facilitates interpretation. However, the loglinear analysis provides chi-square tests for the different hierarchical models, and separate tests of each interaction effect, whereas

TABLE 5.5

Descriptive Statistics for Columns (Age Groups) and Rows
(Type of Disease)

Name	Masses	Coordinates		CONTR		CORR2		Quality
		F1	F2	F1	F2	F1	F2	F1 + F2
Male								
16–25	0.095	0.17	0.17	0.008	0.015	0.243	0.156	0.400
26–35	0.086	0.56	0.14	0.082	0.008	0.773	0.028	0.801
36–45	0.097	0.57	−0.25	0.097	0.031	0.869	0.097	0.966
46–55	0.097	0.57	−0.67	0.096	0.225	0.544	0.447	0.991
55–66	0.062	0.16	−0.51	0.005	0.083	0.084	0.517	0.601
67–100	0.053	−0.66	−0.26	0.072	0.019	0.897	0.083	0.980
Female								
16–25	0.087	−0.11	0.68	0.003	0.205	0.037	0.061	0.898
26–35	0.099	−0.16	0.79	0.008	0.316	0.055	0.795	0.850
36–45	0.113	0.21	0.17	0.016	0.017	0.645	0.247	0.892
46–55	0.094	−0.06	−0.16	0.001	0.013	0.044	0.206	0.250
56–66	0.064	−0.77	−0.14	0.116	0.006	0.940	0.017	0.958
67–100	0.054	−1.73	−0.47	0.495	0.062	0.946	0.042	0.988
Many times a week	0.119	0.49	−0.95	0.088	0.559	0.297	0.663	0.959
Once a week	0.189	0.44	−0.16	0.110	0.024	0.773	0.060	0.833
2–3 a month	0.178	0.36	0.28	0.070	0.073	0.654	0.238	0.892
Once a month	0.135	0.15	0.43	0.009	0.130	0.104	0.544	0.648
More seldom	0.214	−0.13	0.37	0.012	0.151	0.104	0.466	0.570
Never	0.165	−1.18	−0.27	0.711	0.062	0.964	0.030	0.994

correspondence analysis displays how the different categories are related. Each method has different pros and cons, and the main rule for choosing a method is to apply correspondence analysis to large tables and loglinear models to multivariate cross-classifications with relatively few categories.

6. CONCLUSION

Correspondence analysis is primarily a multivariate descriptive method of analysis that presents the relations between rows and columns in a frequency table graphically as points in a common low-dimensional space. According to Lebart, Morineau, and Warwick (1984, p. 162), the following criteria should be satisfied if the advantages of the method are to be exploited to the full:

1. *The data matrix should be large*, making it difficult to discover the structure by means of simple statistical analyses.
2. The variables must be *homogeneous*, so that it is meaningful to calculate distances between the categories.
3. The method is most suitable for data for which the structure is unknown.

Correspondence analysis is a very flexible method. First it imposes few requirements as regards the data themselves and, second, it allows the use of supplementary information. The method is an *exploratory* technique and can thus serve as a useful supplement to other methods based on hypothesis testing, which tend to dominate the analysis tradition in Anglo-American social sciences. Exploratory and confirmatory data analysis should be used parallel to each other much more often, since each has much to give to the other.

Correspondence analysis has given social scientists a very useful method of analysis. The graphical display is very beneficial for communicating complex relations between variables/categories. Furthermore, it complements other new and important methods such as loglinear models, latent class analysis, etc.

The disadvantages of the method are that the distance between the points of different sets is not defined and it does not include significance tests for effects or interactions. It is in this connection especially that loglinear models are a particularly useful supplement to correspondence analysis. Calculating parameter estimates and significance tests for the interaction effects provides a measure of how strongly the different categories and variables are related. Therefore, loglinear models enable us to obtain more information from the results of the correspondence analysis. On the other hand, correspondence analysis provides a plot of how categories are related, and this might be an aid in interpreting complex interactions detected by loglinear analysis.

APPENDIX A: GLOSSARY

Centroid (c): The centroid (center of gravity) is a weighted mean of the row and column profiles. In correspondence analysis the centroid is placed in the origin of the coordinate system.

Chi-Square distances (d): These distances represents the metric in correspondence analysis, and they are calculated separately between row and column profiles. A large d indicates that two profiles are quite different. If the distance from the centroid is large, then the profile point is very different from the average profile. The chi-square distances are calculated between points within each sets of points, so that the distances between points in two separate sets are not defined.

Column profiles (ac): Column profiles are the relative frequencies in each category of the column variable.

Contribution of points to the inertia of dimensions (ca): The contribution of a point to a dimension (absolute contribution) is the proportion of the inertia this point explains. The sum of these contributions within each set of points is equal to 1.00. In interpreting a dimension, the points with the highest values are awarded the greatest importance.

Coordinates (f): These values identify the positions of the points in the p-dimensional space.

Eigenvalues (λ^2): Eigenvalues (characteristic root) indicate how much of the total inertia (variance) each factor explains.

Inertia (Λ^2): Inertia is analogous to the terms variance and eigenvalues. The term *total inertia* refers to the sum of the eigenvalues (trace) and equals Pearson's mean square contingency coefficient.

Masses (r): Masses are the relative frequencies of the row and column totals, and these are used to weight the point profiles. The masses are a measure of a point's importance or influence on the analysis.

Profile elements: The entries of each row and column profile.

Row profiles (ar): Row profiles are the relative frequencies in each category of the row variable.

Singular values (λ): These values are the square roots of the eigenvalues, and may be interpreted as the maximum canonical correlations between the categories of the variables.

Squared correlations (cr): Squared correlations (contributions of dimensions to the inertia of points) indicate how much of the inertia of a point is explained by a factor. These values are independent of the point's mass. The sum of these contributions expresses the goodness of fit of each point's representation in the solution, and is often termed the quality of the description. In the French tradition the squared correlations are called relative contributions.

APPENDIX B: SAS PROGRAM
COMMANDS AND OUTPUT

The SAS program to perform correspondence analysis is called
PROC CORRESP, and both program lines and output for analysis of
Table 2.1 follow:

```
title 'crimes by regions in Norway';
data crime;
  /* Read contingency table */
  input region $ 20. burgl 21-24 fraud 26-29
  vandal 31-35
        dens 37-40 spars 42-44;
  label burgl = 'burglary'
        fraud = 'fraud'
        vandal = 'vandalism'
        dens = 'densely'
        spars = 'sparsely'
        ;
  /* Define Norway as supplementary point */
  if region = 'Norway'
  then w = -1;
  else w = 1;

  cards;
Oslo area          395  2456   1758  749   66
Mid-Norway         147   153    916  235  135
North Norway       694   327   1347  283  185
Norway            4558  5129  10842   .    .
;

  /* Perform simple correspondence analysis */

proc corresp print=percent observed cellchi2 rp
cp
  outc=coor;
  var burgl fraud vandal dens spars;
```

```
  supplementary dens spars;
  id region;
  weight w;
run
;

  /* Create data set for plotting */

data coor;
   set coor;
   y    = dim1;
   x    = dim2;
   xsys = '2';
   ysys = '2';
   text = region;
   size = 1.2;
   label y = 'Dimension 1'
         x = 'Dimension 2';
   keep x y text xsys ysys size;
run;

  /* Plot Correspondence Analysis Results */

proc gplot data = coor;
  symbol v = none;
  axis1 order = -0.6 to 0.6 by 0.6;
  plot x*y = 1 / annotate = coor frame haxis = axis1
vaxis = axis1
  href = 0 vref = 0;
run;
```

Crimes by Regions in Norway
The Correspondence Analysis Procedure
Contingency Table

Percents	Burglary	Fraud	Vandalism	Sum
Oslo area	4.821	29.977	21.457	56.255
Mid Norway	1.794	1.867	11.180	14.842
North Norway	8.471	3.991	16.441	28.903
Sum	15.086	35.835	49.078	100.000

Supplementary Rows

Percents	Burglary	Fraud	Vandalism
Norway	55.633	62.602	132.332

Supplementary Columns

Percents	Dense	Sparse
Oslo area	9.14195	0.80557
Mid Norway	2.86830	0.42719
North Norway	3.45417	1.03747

Contributions to the Total Chi-Square Statistic

Percents	Burglary	Fraud	Vandalism	Sum
Oslo area	7.802	23.560	6.755	38.116
Mid Norway	0.436	11.036	10.269	21.740
North Norway	19.094	19.282	1.768	40.144
Sum	27.331	53.877	18.792	100.000

Row Profiles

Percents	Burglary	Fraud	Vandalism
Oslo area	8.5702	53.2870	38.1428
Mid Norway	12.0888	12.5822	75.3289
North Norway	29.3074	13.8091	56.8834

Supplementary Row Profiles

Percents	Burglary	Fraud	Vandalism
Norway	22.2027	24.9842	52.8131

Column Profiles

Percents	Burglary	Fraud	Vandalism
Oslo area	31.9579	83.6512	43.7205
Mid Norway	11.8932	5.2112	22.7804
North Norway	56.1489	11.1376	33.4991

Supplementary Column Profiles

Percents	Dense	Sparse
Oslo area	59.1160	35.4839
Mid Norway	18.5478	18.8172
North Norway	22.3362	45.6989

The Correspondence Analysis Procedure
Inertia and Chi-Square Decomposition

Singular Values	Principal Inertias	Chi-Squares	Percents	17	34	51	68	85
				----+----+----+----+----+----				
0.42124	0.17744	1453.78	87.44%	**************************				
0.15966	0.02549	208.84	12.56%	****				
	0.20293	1662.63	(Degrees of freedom = 4)					

Row Coordinates

	Dim1	Dim2
Oslo area	−0.370698	0.008999
Mid Norway	0.419906	−0.347745
North Norway	0.505887	0.161056

Supplementary Row Coordinates

	Dim1	Dim2
Norway	0.249926	0.082522

Summary Statistics for the Row Points

	Quality	Mass	Inertia
Oslo area	1.00000	0.562553	0.381160
Mid Norway	1.00000	0.148419	0.271399
North Norway	1.00000	0.289027	0.401441

Quality of Representation for the Supplementary Row Points

Norway	1.00000

Partial Contributions to Inertia for the Row Points

	Dim1	Dim2
Oslo area	0.435659	0.001787
Mid Norway	0.147482	0.704099
North Norway	0.416859	0.294114

Indices of the Coordinates that Contribute Most to Inertia for the Row Points

	Dim1	Dim2	Best
Oslo area	1	0	1
Mid Norway	0	2	2
North Norway	1	1	1

Squared Cosines for the Row Points

	Dim1	Dim2
Oslo area	0.999411	0.000589
Mid Norway	0.593179	0.406821
North Norway	0.907972	0.092028

Squared Cosines for the Supplementary Row Points

	Dim1	Dim2
Norway	0.901696	0.098304

Column Coordinates

	Dim1	Dim2
Burglary	0.511640	0.325379
Fraud	− 0.550442	0.045999
Vandalism	0.244643	− 0.133604

Supplementary Column Coordinates

	Dim1	Dim2
Dense	− 0.067094	− 0.145343
Sparse	0.424134	0.071142

Summary Statistics for the Column Points

	Quality	Mass	Inertia
Burglary	1.00000	0.150860	0.273310
Fraud	1.00000	0.358355	0.538775
Vandalism	1.00000	0.490785	0.187915

Quality of Representation for the Supplementary Column Points

Dense	1.00000
Sparse	1.00000

Partial Contributions to Inertia for the Column Points

	Dim1	Dim2
Burglary	0.222561	0.626579
Fraud	0.611900	0.029746
Vandalism	0.165539	0.343676

Indices of the Coordinates that Contribute Most to Inertia for the Column Points

	Dim1	Dim2	Best
Burglary	2	2	2
Fraud	1	0	1
Vandalism	0	2	2

Squared Cosines for the Column Points

	Dim1	Dim2
Burglary	0.712030	0.287970
Fraud	0.993065	0.006935
Vandalism	0.770272	0.229728

Squared Cosines for the Supplementary Column Points

	Dim1	Dim2
Dense	0.175664	0.824336
Sparse	0.972635	0.027365

APPENDIX C: SPSS PROGRAM
LINES AND OUTPUT

Correspondence analysis is available as an optional extension of the SPSS system called *SPSS Categories*, which contains procedures for both conjoint analysis and optimal scaling. The procedure that performs correspondence analysis is called ANACOR. An example of program lines and output for analysis of Table 4.1 follow:

```
data list free / var1 type1 freq.

value labels
  var1 1 'dwelling' 2 'car' 3 'alcoprobl'
  4 'sedatives' 5 'nervous' 6 'smokes'
  7 'alcocons' 8 'income' 9 'insurance'
  10 'narcotics' 11 'convicted' 12 'bad health'
  13 'daily exp' 14 'nok2000' 15 'low ed'
  16 'unemployed' 17 'longterm' 18 'house debt'
  19 'penalty' 20 'men' 21 'women' 22 '18-24'
  23 '25-30' 24 '30-50' 25 'unmarried'
  26 'married' 27 'divorced' 28 'rural'      .
  29 'urban' 30 'city'/
  type1 1 'SICK' 2 'DEVIANTS' 3 'DEPENDENTS'
  4 'INDEBTED'
  .


  begin data
  1  1   75  1  2   49  1  3   43  1  4  194
  2  1   63  2  2   45  2  3   38  2  4  171
  3  1   24  3  2   47  3  3    1  3  4    2
  4  1  131  4  2   21  4  3   16  4  4   15
  5  1  139  5  2   40  5  3   40  5  4   41
  6  1  137  6  2  114  6  3  106  6  4  159
  7  1   15  7  2   79  7  3    5  7  4    4
  8  1   48  8  2   46  8  3   18  8  4  143
  9  1  124  9  2   51  9  3   64  9  4  124
 10  1    5 10  2   42 10  3   10 10  4    1
 11  1   20 11  2   98 11  3   34 11  4   29
 12  1  132 12  2   42 12  3   37 12  4   53
```

```
13  1    95  13  2    44  13  3    83  13  4    86
14  1   143  14  2    83  14  3   121  14  4   149
15  1   101  15  2    45  15  3    49  15  4    62
16  1    57  16  2    97  16  3    92  16  4    98
17  1    61  17  2    67  17  3   115  17  4    62
18  1    76  18  2    32  18  3    56  18  4   195
19  1     7  19  2    65  19  3    12  19  4     6
20  1    49  20  2   113  20  3    46  20  4   105
21  1   111  21  2    11  21  3    76  21  4    95
22  1    21  22  2    38  22  3    23  22  4    34
23  1    24  23  2    36  23  3    33  23  4    60
24  1   115  24  2    50  24  3    66  24  4   106
25  1    64  25  2    90  25  3    66  25  4    69
26  1    24  26  2     8  26  3    15  26  4    72
27  1    71  27  2    26  27  3    40  27  4    58
28  1    57  28  2    32  28  3    29  28  4    82
29  1    72  29  2    53  29  3    55  29  4    65
30  1    30  30  2    37  30  3    37  30  4    52
end data.
```

```
weight by freq.

anacor table = var1 (1,30) by type1 (1,4) /
  dimension = 2 /
  normalization = canon /
  print = scores contributions/
  plot ndim(1,2) joint.
```

ANACOR-Version 0.4 by Department of Data Theory,
University of Leiden, The Netherlands

Dimension	Singular Value	Inertia	Proportion Explained	Cumulative Proportion
1	0.35123	0.12336	0.537	0.537
2	0.27540	0.07584	0.330	0.868
3	0.17441	0.03042	0.132	1.000
Total		0.22962	1.000	1.000

Row Scores:

VAR1	Marginal Profile	Dim 1	Dim 2
1 Dwelling	0.048	0.451	0.678
2 Car	0.042	0.426	0.708
3 Alcoprob	0.010	− 1.656	− 0.588
4 Sedative	0.024	0.412	− 1.698
5 Nervous	0.035	0.219	− 1.053
6 Smokes	0.069	− 0.049	0.009
7 Alcocons	0.014	− 2.219	− 0.054
8 Income	0.034	0.321	0.812
9 Insuranc	0.048	0.315	− 0.136
10 Narcotic	0.008	− 2.163	0.004
11 Convicte	0.024	− 1.386	0.198
12 Bad heal	0.035	0.225	− 0.858
13 Daily ex	0.041	0.202	− 0.216
14 NOK2000	0.066	0.132	− 0.098
15 Low ed	0.034	0.128	− 0.492
16 Unemploy	0.046	− 0.360	0.223
17 Longterm	0.041	− 0.232	− 0.106
18 House de	0.048	0.610	0.654
19 Penalty	0.012	− 2.104	0.149
20 Men	0.042	− 0.557	0.424
21 Women	0.039	0.654	− 0.333
22 18−24	0.015	− 0.481	0.237
23 25−30	0.020	− 0.088	0.489
24 30−50	0.045	0.257	− 0.199
25 Unmarrie	0.038	− 0.460	− 0.008
26 Married	0.016	0.747	0.822
27 Divorced	0.026	0.304	− 0.306
28 Rural	0.027	0.287	0.185
29 Urban	0.033	− 0.061	− 0.171
30 City	0.021	− 0.135	0.256

Contribution of Row Points to the Inertia of Each Dimension

VAR1	Marginal Profile	Dim 1	Dim 2
1 Dwelling	0.048	0.028	0.080
2 Car	0.042	0.022	0.077
3 Alcoprob	0.010	0.077	0.012
4 Sedative	0.024	0.012	0.255
5 Nervous	0.035	0.005	0.139
6 Smokes	0.069	0.000	0.000
7 Alcocons	0.014	0.192	0.000
8 Income	0.034	0.010	0.081
9 Insuranc	0.048	0.014	0.003
10 Narcotic	0.008	0.103	0.000
11 Convicte	0.024	0.132	0.003
12 Bad heal	0.035	0.005	0.094
13 Daily ex	0.041	0.005	0.007
14 NOK2000	0.066	0.003	0.002
15 Low ed	0.034	0.002	0.030
16 Unemploy	0.046	0.017	0.008
17 Longterm	0.041	0.006	0.002
18 House de	0.048	0.051	0.074
19 Penalty	0.012	0.151	0.001
20 Men	0.042	0.037	0.027
21 Women	0.039	0.048	0.016
22 18–24	0.015	0.010	0.003
23 25–30	0.020	0.000	0.018
24 30–50	0.045	0.008	0.006
25 Unmarrie	0.038	0.023	0.000
26 Married	0.016	0.025	0.039
27 Divorced	0.026	0.007	0.009
28 Rural	0.027	0.006	0.003
29 Urban	0.033	0.000	0.003
30 City	0.021	0.001	0.005
		1.000	1.000

Contribution of Dimensions to the Inertia of Each Row Point

VAR1	Marginal Profile	Dim 1	Dim 2	Total
1 Dwelling	0.048	0.321	0.568	0.889
2 Car	0.042	0.283	0.612	0.895
3 Alcoprob	0.010	0.757	0.075	0.831
4 Sedative	0.024	0.062	0.824	0.886
5 Nervous	0.035	0.050	0.897	0.947
6 Smokes	0.069	0.336	0.009	0.345
7 Alcocons	0.014	0.934	0.000	0.934
8 Income	0.034	0.123	0.618	0.742
9 Insuranc	0.048	0.836	0.121	0.958
10 Narcotic	0.008	0.999	0.000	0.999
11 Convicte	0.024	0.984	0.016	1.000
12 Bad heal	0.035	0.072	0.822	0.893
13 Daily ex	0.041	0.221	0.198	0.419
14 NOK2000	0.066	0.230	0.100	0.330
15 Low ed	0.034	0.079	0.916	0.996
16 Unemploy	0.046	0.442	0.133	0.575
17 Longterm	0.041	0.076	0.012	0.088
18 House de	0.048	0.517	0.466	0.983
19 Penalty	0.012	0.986	0.004	0.990
20 Men	0.042	0.655	0.297	0.952
21 Women	0.039	0.728	0.148	0.875
22 18–24	0.015	0.831	0.158	0.988
23 25–30	0.020	0.036	0.867	0.903
24 30–50	0.045	0.679	0.320	0.999
25 Unmarrie	0.038	0.879	0.000	0.879
26 Married	0.016	0.489	0.465	0.954
27 Divorced	0.026	0.551	0.438	0.989
28 Rural	0.027	0.575	0.187	0.762
29 Urban	0.033	0.083	0.498	0.580
30 City	0.021	0.152	0.432	0.584

Column Scores:

TYPE1	Marginal Profile	Dim 1	2
1 SICK	0.278	0.326	−0.730
2 DEVIANTS	0.213	−1.102	0.093
3 DEPENDEN	0.190	0.013	−0.081
4 INDEBTED	0.319	0.444	0.624

Contribution of Column Points to the Inertia of Each Dimension

TYPE1	Marginal Profile	Dim 1	2
1 SICK	0.278	0.084	0.539
2 DEVIANTS	0.213	0.737	0.007
3 DEPENDEN	0.190	0.000	0.004
4 INDEBTED	0.319	0.179	0.450
		1.000	1.000

Contribution of Dimensions to the Inertia of Each Column Point

TYPE1	Marginal Profile	Dim 1	2	Total
1 SICK	0.278	0.192	0.753	0.945
2 DEVIANTS	0.213	0.980	0.005	0.986
3 DEPENDEN	0.190	0.000	0.014	0.014
4 INDEBTED	0.319	0.382	0.591	0.972

REFERENCES

BENZÈCRI, J.-P. (1969) "Statistical analysis as a tool to make patterns emerge from data," in S. Watanabe (ed.), *Methodologies of Pattern Recognition*, (pp. 35–74). New York: Academic Press.

BENZÈCRI, J.-P. et al. (1973) *Analyse des Données*. Paris: Dunod.

BENZÉCRI, J.-P. (1992) *Correspondence Analysis Handbook*. New York: Dekker.

BOURDIEU, P. (1984) *Distinction. A Social Critique of the Judgement of Taste*. Cambridge, MA: Harvard University Press.

BOURDIEU, P. (1988) *Homo Academicus*. Stanford, CA: Stanford University Press.

CALHOUN, C., LIPUMA, E., and POSTONE, M. (eds.) (1992) *Bourdieu: Critical Perspectives*. Cambridge, UK: Polity Press.

CARROLL, J. D., GREEN, P. E., and SCHAFFER, C. M. (1986) "Interpoint distance comparisons in correspondence analysis." *Journal of Marketing Research* 23: 271–280.

CARROLL, J. D., GREEN, P. E., and SCHAFFER, C. M. (1987) "Comparing interpoint distances in correspondence analysis: A clarification." *Journal of Marketing Research* 24: 445–450.

CATTELL, R. B. (1966) "The scree test for the number of factors." *Multivariate Behavioral Research* 1: 245–276.

CIBOIS, P. (1983) *L'analyse Factorielle*. Paris: Presses Universitaires de France.

CLAUSEN, S.-E. (1996) "A classification of social assistance recipients in Norway." *Scandinavian Journal of Social Welfare* 5: 208–214.

DE LEEUW, J. (1984) *Canonical Analysis of Categorical Data*. Leiden: DSWO Press (Doctoral dissertation, 1973).

FISHER, R. A. (1940) "The precision of discriminant functions." *Annals of Eugenics* 10: 422–429.

FORNELL, C. (ed.) (1982) *A Second Generation of Multivariate Analysis* (Vol. 1: Methods). New York: Praeger.

GIFI, A. (1981) *Non-linear Multivariate Analysis*. Leiden: University of Leiden.

GOODMAN, L. A. (1987) "New methods for analyzing the intrinsic character of qualitative variables using cross-classified data." *American Journal of Sociology* 93(3): 529–583.

GREEN, P. E., and CARROLL, J. D. (1976) *Mathematical Tools for Applied Multivariate Analysis*. New York: Academic Press.

GREENACRE, M. J. (1981) "Practical correspondence analysis," in V. Barnett (ed.) *Interpreting Multivariate Data* (pp. 119–146). New York: Wiley.

GREENACRE, M. J. (1984) *Theory and Applications of Correspondence Analysis*. New York: Academic Press.

GREENACRE, M. J. (1993) *Correspondence Analysis in Practice*. London: Academic Press.

GREENACRE, M. J. (1994) "Correspondence analysis and its interpretation," in M. Greenacre and J. Blasius (eds.), *Correspondence Analysis in the Social Sciences* (pp. 3–22). San Diego, CA: Academic Press.

GREENACRE, M. J., and BLASIUS, J. (eds.) (1994) *Correspondence Analysis in the*

65

66

Social Sciences: Recent Developments and Applications. San Diego, CA: Academic Press.

GUTTMAN, L. (1941) "The quantification of a class of attributes: A theory and method of scale construction," in P. Horst et al. (eds.) *The Prediction of Personal Adjustment* (pp. 319–348). New York: The Social Science Research Council.

GUTTMAN, L. (1950) "The principal components of scale analysis," in S. A. Stouffer et al. (eds.) *Measurement and Prediction* (pp. 312–361). Princeton: Princeton University Press.

GUTTMAN, L. (1959) "Meticizing rank-ordered or unordered data for a linear factor analysis." *Sankhyā* 21: 257–268.

HILL, M. O. (1974) "Correspondence analysis: A neglected multivariate method." *Applied Statistics* 23(3): 340–354.

HIRSCHFELD, H. O. (1935) "A connection between correlation and contingency." *Cambridge Philosophical Society Proceedings* 31: 520–524.

HOFFMAN, D. L., and FRANKE, G. R. (1986) "Correspondence analysis: Graphical representation of categorical data in market research." *Journal of Marketing Research* 23: 213–227.

HOTELLING, H. (1933) "Analysis of a complex of statistical variables into principal components." *Journal of Educational Psychology* 24: 417–441, 498–520.

KNOKE, D., and BURKE, P. J. (1980) *Log-Linear Models.* Sage University Paper series on Quantitative Applications in the Social Sciences, 07-020. Thousand Oaks, CA: Sage.

LAGARDE, J. DE (1983) *Initiation à l'Analyse des Données.* Paris: Dunod.

LEBART, L., MORINEAU, A., and WARWICK, K. M. (1984) *Multivariate Descriptive Statistical Analysis. Correspondence Analysis and Related Techniques for Large Matrices.* New York: Wiley.

MORAN, M. A., and GORNBEIN, J. (1988) "CA—Correspondence Analysis." Technical Report #87, BMDP Statistical Software, Inc., Los Angeles.

NISHISATO, S. (1980) *Analysis of Categorical Data: Dual Scaling and its Applications.* Toronto: University of Toronto Press.

SAS Institute (1989) *SAS / STAT User's Guide*, Version 6, 4th ed. (Vol. 1). Cary, NC: SAS Institute Inc.

SPSS INC. (1990) *SPSS Categories.* Chicago: SPSS.

STATISTICS NORWAY (1986) *Criminal Statistics 1984* (NOS-647). Oslo: Statistics Norway.

STATISTICS NORWAY (1987) *Health Survey 1985* (NOS-692). Oslo: Statistics Norway.

STATISTICS NORWAY (1996) *Survey of Level of Living 1995* (C301). Oslo: Statistics Norway.

TENENHAUS, M., and YOUNG, F. W. (1985) "An analysis and synthesis of multiple correspondence analysis, optimal scaling, dual scaling, homogeneity analysis, and other methods for quantifying categorical multivariate data." *Psychometrika* 50: 91–119.

VAN DER HEIJDEN, P. G. M. (1987) *Correspondence Analysis of Longitudinal Categorical Data.* Leiden: DSWO Press.

VAN DER HEIJDEN, P. G. M., and DE LEEUW, J. (1985) "Correspondence analysis used complementary to loglinear analysis." *Psychometrika* 50(4): 429–447.

VAN DER HEIJDEN, P. G. M., and DE LEEUW, J. (1989) "Correspondence analysis, with special attention to the analysis of panel data and event history data," in C. C. Clogg (ed.), *Sociological Methodology 1989* (pp. 43–87). Oxford: Blackwell.

VAN DER HEIJDEN, P. G. M., MOOIJAART, A., and TAKANE, Y. (1994) "Correspondence analysis and contingency table models," in M. Greenacre and J. Blasius (eds.), *Correspondence Analysis in the Social Sciences* (pp. 79–111). San Diego, CA: Academic Press.

VAN RIJCKESVORSEL, J. (1987) *The Application of Fuzzy Coding and Horseshoes in Multiple Correspondence Analysis*. Leiden: DSWO Press.

WELLER, S. C., and ROMNEY, A. K. (1990) *Metric Scaling: Correspondence Analysis*. Sage University Paper series on Quantitative Applications in the Social Sciences, 07-075. Thousand Oaks, CA: Sage.

YOUNG, F. W. (1984) "Scaling." *Annual Review of Psychology* 35: 55–81.

ABOUT THE AUTHOR

STEN-ERIK CLAUSEN is Senior Researcher at the Norwegian Institute for Urban and Regional Research. He has also taught social psychology and quantitative methods courses at the University of Oslo, Norway. He is a social psychologist, with a background in psychometrics. His special interests include studies of deviant behavior and marginalization. He has published articles on drug abuse and welfare clients. His research interests also include multivariate methods and its applications in the social sciences.